CELEBRATING SILENCE

His Holiness
Sri Sri Ravi Shankar

Excerpts from
Five Years of Weekly Knowledge
1995-2000

Edited by
Bill Hayden and Anne Elixhauser

CELEBRATING SILENCE
BY SRI SRI RAVI SHANKAR

Published by
Art of Living Foundation
Post Office Box 50003
Santa Barbara, California 93150
(877) 399-1008 (U.S. toll free)
(805) 564-1002
Printed in the United States of America

ISBN 1-885289-39-1

Edited by Bill Hayden and Anne Elixhauser
Cover Design: Bill Herman
Production Support: Laura Weinberg

OTHER WORKS BY THE AUTHOR

Wisdom for the New Millennium
God Loves Fun
Waves of Beauty
Bang on the Door

Talks published singly:

The Language of the Heart
Prayer, the Call of the Soul
The Way Back Home
You Are the Blue Sky

The teachings of Sri Sri Ravi Shankar are available in
the form of books, video recordings and audiotapes.
For a catalog of products and to order, contact:

Art of Living Books and Tapes
(800) 574-3001 U.S.A. or (641) 472-9892
Fax: (641) 472-0671
E-mail: aolmailorder@lisco.com

In June of 1995, His Holiness Sri Sri Ravi Shankar began a weekly tradition of creating a short talk, often on a subject that was relevant to current events. Each week this knowledge flows by electronic mail, by fax and by post all around the world, to every continent, and each year these talks have been compiled into volumes. This is a collection of excerpts from these talks from the first five years.

Whether reading a talk from years past or hearing a current one for the first time, the knowledge is always fresh and meaningful. Those who are lucky enough to be with Sri Sri when the knowledge is created, discover truths that fill both the heart and the intellect. In his words, "Being with the Guru means spontaneous integration of life and wisdom."

People often feel that the current weekly knowledge applies to an immediate need and there are many instances where someone seeking wisdom or advice, picked up a volume and opened it randomly to find exactly what they required at that moment. The paradigm of time, space and separateness breaks down.

The journey for this collection began in New Delhi and ended in Rishikesh, India. The voyage in between included many passages around the world, during which many hearts and minds were blessed with the wisdom of this humble man.

This collection is thematic rather than chronological. The first chapter helps us understand the more concrete issues that we deal with, such as anger, doubt and fear – those things we want to change, as well as love and dispassion – those things we want to culture. The second chapter, building on the first, educates us on what it means to be on a spiritual path, discussing service, spiritual practices and surrender. The third chapter is most sublime, leading us through an understanding of God, our relationship to Him, and back to our inner Self – that which we really seek, often without knowing.

*Y*our inability to do something, such as break a habit, causes a pinch and when you are deeply pained by something, the pain will rid you of that habit. If you are pained by your shortcomings, then you are a sadhak – a seeker. Pain takes you out of addiction.

Los Angeles, California, United States
January 30, 1997

*I*f you cannot eliminate vices, magnify them. Worry, pride, anger, lust, grief – give them a bigger dimension and a different direction. What is the point of getting angry about small events? Be angry about the infinite, about Brahma. If you cannot get rid of pride, take pride in owning the Divine. If you are bothered by greed, be greedy for satsang. If cravings gnaw at you, crave the truth. If jealousy haunts you, be jealous about seva. Be averse to aversions. Attach yourself to the guru. Get intoxicated with the Divine.

Rishikesh, India
April 3, 1997

*D*esires for sensory pleasure are electric in nature and these desires get neutralized as they move towards the object of your senses.

If, by your skill, you could move your desires deeper within you towards the center of your existence, another dimension of everlasting pleasure, thrill, bliss and undying love will be yours. Lust, greed, power and jealousy are powerful because they are nothing but energy and you are the source of it – the pure electricity. Dedication and devotion maintain the purity of your electricity, moving you upward.

Once you realize that you are pleasure or electricity, your cravings subside and serenity dawns. Remembering that you will die makes you alive now and frees you from cravings and aversions.

Milano, Italy
January 7, 1998

*D*esire kills joy yet the goal of all desires is joy. Whenever happiness has disappeared from your life, look deep within and you will see it is because of desire.

Yet all that we desire is happiness. No creature desiring unhappiness is ever born; never has it happened before and never will it happen in the future.

When your small mind gets tired of running here and there, of wandering everywhere, it reaches the conclusion, "My desires have killed my happiness."

Bangalore Ashram, India
April 26, 2000

*A*ll desires are for happiness. That is the goal of desire, isn't it? But how often does your desire lead you to the goal? Have you thought about the nature of desire? It simply means tomorrow, and not now. But joy is never tomorrow; it is always now.

How can you have desires when you are joyful? And how can you really be joyful right now when you have desires? Desire appears to lead you to happiness, but in fact it cannot. That is why desire is maya – illusion.

Bangalore Ashram, India
March 6, 1996

*H*ow does a desire arise? A desire arises with the memory of a pleasant experience or with past impressions. A desire might also arise through listening. A desire can be triggered through association with certain people or certain places. Someone else's need or desire may manifest in you as your own desire. When someone is hungry, you might have a desire to feed them, or if someone wants to talk with you, a spontaneous desire may arise in you to talk with them.

Destiny, or a happening in which you have a part to play, may trigger a desire but you will not be aware of the reason for your actions. For example, a gentleman in Quebec, Canada built roads and worked on a farm for 30 years, not knowing for what – the farm was destined to become our Montreal Ashram and the roads he built are the roads we use now.

Dharamshala, Himachal Pradesh, India
April 6, 2000

*D*esires arise on their own without asking you. And when they come, what do you do with them? If you say that you do not want any desires, then that want becomes another desire.

Here is a clue for you: if you want to go to a movie, you have to buy a ticket and this ticket must be given to the doorman. If you hold onto the ticket, how can you go in? Similarly, if you want to be admitted to college, you must complete an application form and submit it. You cannot hold onto it.

Likewise on the journey of life, you have to keep submitting your desires and not hold onto them. As you keep submitting your desires, then fewer desires arise.

Unfortunate are those who keep on desiring yet their desires are not fulfilled. A little more fortunate are those whose desires get fulfilled over a long period of time. More fortunate are those whose desires get fulfilled as soon as they arise. The most fortunate are those who have no desires because there is fulfillment even before the desire arises.

Swargashram (Heavenly Abode), Rishikesh, India
March 20, 1996

*B*uddha said that desire is the cause of all misery. If your desire does not get fulfilled, it leads to frustration and causes misery. And if your desire does get fulfilled, it leaves you empty.

Vasishta said that desire is the cause of pleasure. You get pleasure from an object or a person only when you desire them. When you do not desire an object, you will not get pleasure from it. When you are hot and thirsty, a sip of cold water gives you pleasure; but there is no pleasure if you are not thirsty. Whatever gives you pleasure, binds you and bondage is misery.

I tell you, when you desire truth, all other desires drop off. You always desire something that is not there but truth is always there. Desire for truth removes all other desires; then it dissolves and what remains is bliss.

Denpasar, Bali, Indonesia
May 11, 2000

*Y*our desires and sankalpas – or intentions – separate you from God. Offer all your desires and all your sankalpas to the Divine. Then you are divine. You are God. You are free – lacking nothing.

Bangalore Ashram, India
October 16, 1996

*P*leasure and pain are intense sensations in this body. When we are not caught up in pleasure or pain, we can truly and sincerely say, "I belong to you." That is when all cravings and aversions, desires and doubts fall off – and in a moment the world belongs to you.

All your miseries surround the "I, I, I, . . ." – "I want this, I like that, I do not like this." Just let go. Remember – the sun rises and sets, the grass grows, the river flows, the moon shines and I am here forever.

European Ashram, Bad Antogast, Germany
May 14, 1997

*K*rishna means the most attractive. He is the divinity, the energy that attracts everything to it. Krishna is the formless center that is everywhere. All attractions from anywhere come only from Krishna.

Often people fail to see the spirit behind the attraction and merely hold onto the outer shell. And the moment you try to possess the shell, you will see Krishna has played a trick and you will be left with an empty shell in your hands and tears in your eyes.

Do not be tricked by Krishna – be clever like Radha. Krishna could not escape from Radha because her whole world was filled with Krishna. If you can see that wherever there is an attraction there is Krishna, then you are Radha, you are in your center.

The mind moves towards beauty, joy and truth. Krishna tells Arjuna, "I am the beauty in the Beautiful, the strength in the Strong, the wisdom in the Wise." In this way he arrests the mind from moving away from him.

Rotterdam, Netherlands
August 16, 1995

*A*ttachments cause feverish breath. Feverish breath takes away your peace of mind. And without peace of mind, you come apart and fall prey to misery. Unfortunately most people do not notice this until it is too late. Before you get scattered too much, gather yourself together and rid your breath of feverishness through surrender and sadhana – spiritual practices.

When you are drowning in the ocean of attachments, surrender is a life jacket. Without fighting attachments, observe your feverish breath and go to the cool place of silence within. Your first step in this direction is directing your attachment to knowledge, to the Divine.

Your non-attachment to the mundane is your charm. Your attachment to the Divine is your beauty.

Sydney, Australia
April 3, 1996

*C*raving comes from encouraging thoughts of pleasure. Yet the actual experience of pleasure may not be as pleasurable as the memory of it. Whether you encourage a worldly thought or a Divine thought, they both bring you pleasure. Worldly thoughts lead to indulgence, which brings you down from pleasure to disappointment and dejection. Divine thoughts take you up from pleasure to bliss, intelligence and progress in life. Worldly thoughts bring pleasure only as memory, while Divine thoughts come as reality.

Question: "What is a Divine thought?"

I am not the body; I am bliss, satchitananda; I am unbounded space; I am love; I am peace; I am light.

Question: "What is a worldly thought?"

Worldly thoughts are about money, sex, food, power, status and self-image.

Truth is hidden by the golden veil of the mundane. Pierce through this thin glittering sheath and know you are the sun.

Montreal Ashram, Quebec, Canada
July 2, 1997

*I*n love even an object is elevated to life. Stones and trees speak to you; the sun, the moon, the entire creation become alive and divine. In lust even a living being becomes a mere object.

- Lust brings tension; love brings relaxation.

- In lust there is cunning and manipulation; in love there is playfulness.

- Lust focuses on a part; love focuses on the whole.

- In lust you want to grasp and possess; in love you want to give and surrender.

- In lust there is effort; love is effortless.

- Lust brings violence; love brings sacrifice.

- Lust demands; love commands.

- In lust you are confused; in love you are focused.

- Lust is dark and monotonous; love has many modes and colors.

- Lust says, "All I want you to have is what I want." Love says, "I want you to have what you want."

- Lust causes feverishness and frustration; love causes longing and pain.

- Lust imprisons and destroys; love liberates and sets you free.

If someone's lust is interrupted, they become angry and start hating. Hatred in the world today is not out of love; it is out of lust.

Shiva, the embodiment of innocence and love, was meditating. His meditation was disturbed by an arrow of flowers from the lord of lust. As soon as Shiva awoke, he opened his third eye and the lord of lust, Manmathava – one who churns the mind – was reduced to ashes.

Rishikesh, India
March 4, 1999

13

*L*ust grips the mind, tires the body and dulls the intellect. Lust when indulged brings inertia, and when suppressed brings anger. Lust is nothing but primordial unharnessed energy. The same energy when harnessed manifests as enthusiasm, sparkle, sharpness of intellect and love.

What can you do to sublimate lust and transform it into love?

- ◆ Take cold-water baths.

- ◆ Moderate your intake of food.

- ◆ Undertake creative challenges.

- ◆ Be playful. People who are in the grip of lust cannot be genuinely playful. When you are playful, then there is no lust.

- ◆ Be generous. When you realize that you are here only to give, then lust is sublimated. Lust makes you possessive and greedy.

- ◆ Remember death.

- ◆ Be in love with the Divine.

Cochin, India
December 3, 1997

*B*ecause fear is love standing upside down, everything that can be interpreted with love can also be interpreted with fear. A child clinging to its mother can be understood in both ways – the child clings out of love or out of fear. This primal instinct of fear can be totally transformed through awareness of Divine love.

Fear is an impression of the past reflecting the future of the present. When people deny fear, they become egocentric; when they recognize and accept fear, they go beyond it – they become free from it.

Total lack of fear is possible only in utter chaos or in utmost orderliness. Neither a saint nor a fool has fear, but everywhere in between there is fear. Fear is essential to preserve orderliness in the world. It is a primal instinct.

Fear of death preserves life.
Fear of wrong maintains right.
Fear of sickness encourages hygiene.
Fear of misery makes you righteous.

A child has a pinch of fear so it is careful and alert while walking. A pinch of fear is necessary to keep things moving smoothly. Do not try to eliminate fear. Just meditate and know that you are nobody or that you belong to someone special.

Rishikesh, India
April 10, 1997

15

*W*henever a boundary is broken, it creates some fear. This fear creates aversion; this aversion in turn brings you back inside the boundary, and to keep yourself in the boundary, you set up defenses. But when you try to defend your position, it becomes a stress and every time you work to defend your position it makes you weaker.

On the path, people use even knowledge as a defense against criticism. Do not use knowledge as a defense. Knowledge is like an umbrella for you – a shelter, not a weapon. Of course, sometimes "do not use knowledge as a weapon" becomes an excuse not to be in knowledge.

I say, drop all your defenses. Anyone can make a mistake – even you. Do not defend your mistakes; just accept them and move on. When you are totally defenseless, that is when you will be completely strong.

Bangalore Ashram, India
February 18, 1999

*W*anting to correct a mistake brings doership and doership is the foundation for mistakes. Those who try to correct mistakes get caught up in more mistakes, but those who recognize them are freed.

When you acknowledge a mistake, you try to justify it without taking responsibility for it. And sometimes you accept that you made a mistake but you feel guilty about it. Mistakes are dropped when you are troubled by your conscience – viveka – or when you experience grief.

There may be flaws in any action, any situation or any person. Treat a flaw as you would treat a flower. Just as a flower has to wither away with time, so does a flaw.

Bangalore Ashram, India
October 2, 1998

A devotee asked, "Please forgive me if I have committed a mistake." Why should you be forgiven? You ask for forgiveness because you feel a pinch and you want to be free from it, isn't it? Let the pinch be there. The pinch will not let the mistake happen again. Forgiveness removes the pinch and then you keep repeating it.

But how do you know a mistake is a mistake? A mistake is something that gives you a pinch. It is the pinch that pricks the consciousness and that pinch will not allow the mistake to be repeated. Be with the pinch and not the guilt. It is a very fine balance. Guilt is about a specific action but a pinch is about a specific result or happening. You can only feel guilty about what you did – not about what happened outside you. But whatever happened, whether because of you or someone else, it can cause a pinch in you.

You can get beyond guilt through wisdom – by knowing the nature of mind, the nature of consciousness and by having a broader perspective of the phenomenon. You can learn from your mistakes. But learning is at an intellectual level while you feel the pinch at an emotional level. The drive of your emotions is much stronger than your intellect, so a pinch will not let the mistake recur. But you cannot be driven by your emotions alone. Your intellect acts as a brake for your emotions.

Feel the pinch. The pinch will create an awareness that what happened was beyond your capacity. This awareness will bring you to surrender and surrender will free you from guilt. So the steps of evolution are from pinch to awareness to surrender to freedom.

Bangalore Ashram, India
February 17, 2000

18

*B*lessed are those who do not see a mistake as a mistake. It is hard not to see your own mistake. Outwardly you may justify yourself or try to prove your innocence to someone else, but a mistake pricks the conscience. Do not justify yourself. Instead, feel the prick of the mistake. That very pinch will take you out of the mistake.

A mistake is something that brings misery to you in the long run. So why would someone knowingly commit a mistake? When you point out someone else's mistake, do you consider him to be separate from you? Do you go on pointing out his error or do you make him feel a part of you? When you point out a mistake to someone, does it make him more stressed? Or does it create more awareness in him? Often you do not point out someone's mistake when it is required but not pointing out a mistake – with due consideration to time and place – is also a mistake.

When you make a new mistake, it is not a mistake. Instead, you have learned a valuable lesson. But when you keep doing it over and over again, that is a mistake. A mistake simply means you have missed understanding a lesson that has come your way. Do not lament over your mistake. Just learn a lesson from it. You will not be judged by your mistakes but by your virtues. Mistakes are of the earth. Virtues are of the Divine.

Wise is the one who learns from another's mistakes. Less wise is the one who learns only from his own mistakes. The fool keeps making the same mistakes again and again and never learns from them.

Singapore
February 12, 1998

19

Once somebody made a mistake and Sri Sri asked him, "What punishment can I give you?"

The person replied, "Do not punish me, Guruji, I won't make the mistake again."

After some time, Sri Sri asked another person who had made a mistake, "And what punishment can I give you?"

With a bright smile he replied, "Any punishment, Guruji."

At this Sri Sri turned to the rest of us with a smile and said, "See, he is so confident of my love for him that he is not afraid of any punishment."

Where there is love, there is no fear. Do not be afraid of being punished by God. Trust in the love that He has for you.

Bangalore Ashram, India
September 9, 1999

*D*oubt cannot come where there is a sense of closeness. Doubt needs distance to appear. You never doubt something that is dear to you, close to you. The moment you doubt something, it is no longer dear to you; a distance has come. You may doubt yourself, but you do not doubt that which is yours. Self-doubt is a lack of closeness to oneself. Belonging, closeness and intimacy are all antidotes for doubt.

Rishikesh, India
March 11, 1999

*D*oubt is a gray area. Gray is neither black nor white. Doubt means you want to get rid of something. It is a temporary state. It is neither up nor down and that is where tension arises.

So how do you eliminate doubt? An event, knowledge or conventional wisdom cannot help. What can help? Accept what you doubt as either black or white. Make it black and accept it or make it white and accept that, regardless if it is black or white or something in between. See the gray as just a shade of black or white. Either way, you accept it. Honest or dishonest – accept it. Then the mind is quiet and you are no longer in the gray area.

Montreal Ashram, Quebec, Canada
July 20, 1995

*D*ecision comes only when there is confusion. When there is no confusion, there is no decision. If there is a piece of wood and a biscuit on your desk, do you decide which one to eat?

Decision is always about choice and choice is always confusing. So, all decision makers are confused. Are you confused, decided or happy? When you are confused there is no freedom.

Action is spontaneous when there is no actor. In you, there is an actor and there is a witness. An actor is either confused or decisive, but the witness smiles and realizes that the action is spontaneous.

The more decisions you make, the more confused you are, and as a result you swing between pain and pleasure. The more the witness grows in you, the more playful and untouched you are. Trust, faith, love and joy all manifest in and around you.

Hamburg, Germany
April 29, 1998

*Y*ou ask, "What am I here for?" I tell you, find out what you are not here for.

- ♦ You are not here to blame.
- ♦ You are not here to cry.
- ♦ You are not here to sleep.
- ♦ You are not here to boast.
- ♦ You are not here to fight.
- ♦ You are not here to be angry.
- ♦ You are not here to be miserable.
- ♦ You are not here to worry.

Jakarta, Indonesia
April 10, 1996

*W*hen a worldly man is miserable, he blames the people around him, the system and the world in general. When a seeker is miserable, he blames the world, but in addition he blames the path, the knowledge and himself.

It is better not to be a seeker so that you blame less. But then a seeker – a sadhak – has much more enjoyment. And when there is more joy, the contrast is greater. There is more love in life and more pain. A certain level of maturity is needed to see things as they are and not blame the path, the self and the world.

Bangalore Ashram, India
March 26, 1996

*W*hen someone blames you, what do you usually do? You blame them back or you set up some resistance in yourself. But when someone blames you, they actually take away some negative karma from you. If you understand this and resist yet actually feel happy about it, then all your resistance drops away. And when you drop your resistance, your karma goes away.

So when someone blames you and you resist them, even if you do not react externally, then you are not allowing them to take the negative karma. On the other hand, you may resist on the outside, but if on the inside you do not resist, you will feel immediately lighter.

How do you feel when someone blames you? Do you feel some heaviness? Do you feel hurt, unhappy or sad? This is all because you are resisting. That is it: what you resist persists.

The ignorant person tells someone, "Do not blame me because it will hurt me." They warn you not to blame them because it will hurt them and they will do something harmful to you in revenge. But an enlightened person says, "Do not blame me because it will hurt you." They say this out of compassion.

Braunlage, Germany
August 10, 1995

*N*ormally, you offer your anger freely and your smile rarely. In ignorance, anger is cheap and a smile is costly. In knowledge, a smile is free like the sun, air and water, and anger is extremely expensive like a diamond. Make your smile cheaper and your anger expensive.

Bangalore Ashram, India
September 25, 1996

*N*egativity cannot remain without a hook to hang on. Positivity and happiness can exist without any reason.

The mind goes on trying to find a hook for its negativity – if not this person, then that thing or that person. This perpetuates maya. The creeping vine of negativity needs support in order to grow. But negativity or aversion for even one person can guarantee a one-way ticket to hell – you need nothing else.

Negativity is an indicator for you to move to your center and to broaden your vision to cosmic intelligence. Instead of focusing your attention on a hook for your negativity, look at the seed of the negativity. With meditation, silence and Kriya, the source of negativity is nipped at the root.

Bangalore Ashram, India
September 9, 1999

*D*o you welcome all that comes to you or do you resist everything? If you cannot resist anything, you cannot welcome anything. You cannot resist everything and you cannot welcome everything.

You do not welcome all thoughts that come to your mind. When you welcome a thought, it means you find it good and act on it. If you act on all thoughts that come to your mind, you will end up in a mental hospital or in prison. So, you resist or ignore some thoughts and you welcome other thoughts. You need discrimination in life. Welcoming and resisting are part of the swing in life. Welcoming is essential for expansion and growth, and resistance is essential for maintenance.

Question: "But what you resist persists!"

If you resist a cold, it does not persist. If there is no resistance in your body, you cannot survive. Your body resists some things and welcomes other things.

Where resistance is weak, persistence results. Weak resistance makes opposition persist. A strong resistance erases the opposition. Strong resistance leads to valor, power and samadhi – equanimity. It creates in you the strength of a warrior. Nothing can tempt you; nothing can obstruct you and victory is gained without fighting. Where there is strong resistance or total acceptance, victory is gained without any fighting.

European Ashram, Bad Antogast, Germany
January 21, 1999

*W*hen you are in a harmonious environment your mind picks up any excuse to be in conflict. In this situation, small things are often enough to create tremendous turmoil. And when you are in a contentious environment you tend to seek harmony. Ask yourself this question: Do you seek harmony in every situation or do you seek to widen the differences and prove your righteousness?

When your survival is at stake, you do not complain that nobody loves you. But when you are safe and secure you start demanding attention. Many people create conflict in order to get attention. The seed of negativity and the tendency for conflict in you can only be annihilated by sadhana – spiritual practices.

Kuala Lumpur, Malaysia
November 14, 1996

*O*nly speak knowledge. Do not repeat anything bad that someone tells you about someone else. When someone comes to tell you negative things, discourage them. Do not believe it.

If someone blames you directly, do not believe it. Just know that they are taking away your bad karma and let it go. If you are one of the master's close ones, you will take all the blame of the world with a smile.

Conflict is the nature of the world; comfort is the nature of the Self. Amidst the conflict seek the comfort. Trying to end conflict prolongs it. Face the conflict by seeking the comfort of the Self.

When you are bored with comfort, enjoy the games of the world. When you are tired of the games of the world, enjoy the comforts of the Self. If you are one of the master's close ones, you do both simultaneously.

God is alive in the world and has tolerated all the ongoing conflicts throughout the ages. If God can put up with all the conflicts, you can too. The moment you agree to be with the conflict, it disappears.

People who love peace do not want to fight, and those who fight do not love peace. Those who want peace want to run away. What is needed is to be peaceful within and then fight. This is the whole message of the Bhagavad Gita. Krishna tells Arjuna to fight but to be in peace at the same time.

In the world, you resolve one conflict and another one arises. The conflicts in Russia are solved and then conflicts in Bosnia arise. You make one better and then another starts up. Your body gets a cold, then you get better; then your back hurts and then it gets better. Your body gets better and then the mind goes. Without any intention, misunderstandings happen and conflicts arise. It is not up to you to try to resolve the misunderstandings. Ignore them and be alive.

Toronto, Ottawa, Canada
July 4, 1995

*C*ertain types of people are soft but their softness comes from a lack of courage and forcefulness. People whose softness comes from a lack of courage suffer greatly and eventually become volatile. There is another type of softness in people – a softness that comes out of maturity, magnanimity and the knowledge of the Self.

Similarly there are two types of forcefulness in people – aggression or assertiveness. Some people are forceful in an aggressive manner out of weakness or fear. Others are forceful or assertive out of caring and love, out of compassion. So look into yourself and become aware of what type of softness and what type of forcefulness is in you.

European Ashram, Bad Antogast, Germany
April 15, 1998

*A*ggression and assertiveness overshadow intuition. Often people who are sensitive tend to become aggressive in order to avoid being hurt and in this process, they lose touch with their fine intuition. Fine intuition needs sensitivity, but sensitivity is often painful. In order to avoid pain they become aggressive and assertive, and in turn they lose their intuitive ability.

Intuition is close to the truth. Often aggression and assertiveness thrive on the idea of truthfulness – aggressive people are convinced of the rightness of their position. To be truthful, you do not need to be aggressive or assertive.

Vanprastha Ashram, Rishikesh, India
March 9, 2000

*V*iolence brings noise while nonviolence happens in silence. People who are violent make tremendous noise; they make their violence known, while people who are nonviolent are quiet. But the time has come for the nonviolent ones to make noise so that violence will decrease. The message of nonviolence must come loud and clear so that it can be heard at a young age.

Anger and violence must be associated with shame. Violence in young people comes from a sense of pride in anger and violence, not a sense of shame. People feel proud that they are violent or angry. They think it is prestigious or a status symbol to be aggressive. Some movies and some music promote aggression and violence, and when these are promoted, human values diminish. We must promote human values – especially love, compassion and belongingness – loudly and clearly.

Apple Valley, California, United States
April 21, 1999

*L*ife is a war. Doctors fight against disease. Lawyers fight against injustice. Teachers fight against ignorance.

Depression happens when you lose the will to fight. Arjuna was depressed; he did not want to fight. His bow fell from his hands and his fingers trembled but Krishna urged him to wake up and fight. The decision to fight can take away your depression.

Bangalore Ashram, India
October 6, 1999

*L*ack of idealism is the main cause of depression among young people today. Life appears to be so meaningless to these children, who are either too scared of the competitive world or bogged down by too much stimulation. They need inspiration, and spirituality is that inspiration.

Depression sets in if there is a lack of zeal to fight. Aggression is the antidote to depression. Depression is lack of energy; anger and aggression are bolts of energy.

When Arjuna was depressed, Krishna inspired him to fight and thus breathed life back into him. If you are depressed, do not take Prozac – just fight for any cause.

If aggression crosses a certain limit, it leads you back into depression. That is what happened when King Ashoka won the Kalinga War but became depressed. He had to take refuge in Buddha.

Wise are those who do not fall either into aggression or depression. That is the golden rule of a yogi. Just wake up and acknowledge you are a yogi.

Indore, India
November 26, 1999

*D*eath brings you in touch with the reality of life. Death creates a vacuum, a void and this void is fertile ground for the spirit to manifest. All talents, inventions and creativity spring forth from the void; creation has a tendency to return to the void. All places of worship in all religions are connected with places of burial or cremation because only the awareness of death can bring dispassion and can ground you in knowledge.

According to Indian mythology, Shiva abides in both Mount Kailasa and in Smashana. Kailasa means "where there is only celebration" and Smashana is the cremation ground – "where there is only void." Divinity dwells in the void as well as in celebration. In you there is void; in you there is celebration.

Rishikesh, India
November 18, 1999

*W*ake up and see your life is too short. The realization that life is short will bring dynamism to your life – unwanted things and distractions will fall away. When you must act or make an effort, know that life is short. Time is running out.

What are you doing with your life? Is your life useful to you and the world around you? Realize that life is too short. When you realize life is short, procrastination falls away.

But when you know there are many lifetimes, you realize that if you do not get it sooner, you will get it later. Wake up! Life is eternal!

When you want to enjoy the fruit of action, know that life is eternal. When it comes to hope, you should know that there are many lifetimes. The ignorant person does it the other way – he hurries for the result and is impatient. But impatience disappears when you know that life is eternal. When you expect someone to return a favor or you expect a result from your good deed, you want it quickly. When you expect a result, you are often frustrated. When you are in a hurry, you cannot enjoy. Know that life is eternal.

If someone takes advantage of you or does not thank you, thank them because they will pay you back later with interest. No one should feel remorse that they have been exploited or are unappreciated. When it comes to enjoying the fruit of your actions, good deeds or blessings, know that life is eternal.

Santa Barbara, California, United States
April 28, 1999

34

*M*emory makes you miserable or wise. Memories of events and experiences of the changing finite world bind you but memory of your nature liberates you. Memories of the ever-changing relative – however good or bad – bring bondage. Memory of the non-changing self elevates awareness. Memories of past events and worldly concerns constrict the vastness of the Self. It is all a matter of where you are, of what you are. If you are ignorant, it is because of your memory. If you are enlightened, it is because of your memory.

Forgetfulness of the infinite is misery. Forgetfulness of the trivial is ecstasy.

Question: "How do we let go of unpleasant memories and limitations?"

Know the impermanent nature of the world and events. Know that past events do not exist in the present. Accept the past as it was. Be dispassionate and centered. Do service to the noble. Increase prana – the vital breath, the force of life. Be in the presence of Divine company. Go to the moon.

Bangalore Ashram, India
November 27, 1997

*W*hen you are miserable, know that you have gone away from the Self. This is called ashaucha – becoming unclean.

In India when someone dies, the close relatives are said to be ashaucha for 10 days because they are very sad. They are impure because they have moved away from the Self. After 10 days of just being with that experience and reading the Bhagavad Gita, being with the knowledge and pulling themselves back into the Self, they become shaucha. They have purged the impurities that arose during those events.

This happens again and again in life. You become ashaucha and then you must get back to shaucha. Go deeper into yourself; then real shaucha happens.

Shaucha's benefits are clarity in the intellect, a pleasing mind, focused awareness, control over the senses and eligibility to realize the Self.

Shaucha is disinterest in the tendencies of your own senses and a sense of nonassociation with other people. If some tendency arises in your body just have the understanding, "Oh yes, here is this old familiar tendency again. Come on, I have had this experience enough, and still my body craves for it again." Become disinterested in your own body – this is just an idea, a sort of distaste – and in one moment it changes.

Why do people love each other so much, have such an intimate relationship, and then fight? Ashaucha has happened. If you do not have distaste for the tendency of the senses, then distaste for the object of the senses will come and you will blame the object.

When ashaucha happens, quickly come back to shaucha. Suppose you feel drowned in any worldly aspect, just know this is ashaucha – "That is why I am miserable." Then come back to shaucha.

Your attraction or craving can exist only as long as you think someone is "other." When you think they are part of you or your Self, then the attraction dies out. That is why a husband or a wife may not be attracted to their partner but to someone else because their partner has already become a part of them. When you realize everyone is part of your Self, you enjoy the whole world without a sense of craving.

New Delhi, India
November 9, 1995

*W*hen you share your misery, it will not diminish. When you fail to share your joy, it diminishes. Share your problems only with the Divine, not with anyone else, as that will only increase the problems. Share your joy with everyone.

Question: "How do we help people who share their misery with us?"

Listen to others; yet do not listen. If your mind gets stuck in their problems, not only are they miserable, but you also become miserable.

Honolulu, Hawaii, United States
February 26, 1997

*T*he mind lives on "more." Misery starts with "more and more," and misery makes you dense and gross.

The Self is subtle. To go from gross to subtle you must go through the finest level of the relative – the atom. To overcome aversion, hatred, jealousy, attraction or entanglements, you have to take yourself to the atom. Taking yourself to the atom means accepting a tiny bit of all of this.

It may be difficult to accept something you do not like but you can definitely accept a tiny bit of it – an atom. The moment you accept that one atom, you will see change happen. But this must be done in a meditative state.

Suppose you love someone. You want more and more of them, yet there is no fulfillment. In anu vrat – the vow of an atom – you take just one atom of that person and that is enough to bring fulfillment to you. Though the river is vast, a little sip quenches your thirst. Though the earth has so much food, just a small bite satisfies your hunger. All that you need are tiny bits. Accept a tiny bit of everything in life – that will bring you fulfillment.

European Ashram, Bad Antogast, Germany
August 11, 1999

*E*ach experience brings completeness. Completion means being led to void or nothing. In the progression of life, you will leave behind every experience saying, "This is nothing." Anything that is completed loses its importance. It leads you to void – it is nothing.

A sign of intelligence is how soon you arrive at this understanding. Examine everything in life and say, "This is nothing" and what remains is love, and that is everything. When "this is nothing" does not come out of knowledge, it will come out of misery. Either through knowledge or through misery, you come to the point of "this is nothing, this is nothing." The choice of how you come to that point is yours.

Bangalore Ashram, India
May 4, 2000

*T*he only thing you must remember is how fortunate you are. When you forget this, you become sad. Sorrow reflects your negative qualities and your attachment to your positive qualities. When you think you are not good enough, you blame yourself and you become sad. When you think you are too good, you blame the world, and then again you become sad. The purpose of sorrow is to bring you back to the Self. And the Self is all joy. But coming back to the Self is possible only through knowledge – through awareness.

Knowledge or awareness leads sorrow towards the Self. Without knowledge, the same sorrow multiplies and does not get completed. Knowledge completes sorrow. With the power of knowledge you transcend sorrow.

In this path you have everything. You have this beautiful knowledge that has all flavors – wisdom, laughter, seva, silence, singing, dancing, humor, celebration, yagyas, caring, complaints, problems, complications – and chaos to add color.

Bangalore Ashram, India
October 5, 1995

*I*t is only through merit that you can have faith. When you lack faith, there can be no happiness in either the inner or the outer world. Happiness springs from faith and in forgetting the body consciousness. Pain or sorrow is holding on to body consciousness. When you are happy, you do not feel the body and when you are miserable, you have aches and pains.

Question: "Then why in guided meditation is the attention taken to various parts of the body?"

For an arrow to go forward, it must be pulled back. In the same way when you take your attention to the various parts of the body, that process frees you from body consciousness.

New Delhi, India
November 28, 1996

*I*f you are unhappy, check if any of these are lacking: tapas, or penance; vairagya, or dispassion; sharanagati, or surrender.

Tapas is agreeing with the moment, a total acceptance of pleasant or unpleasant situations. Vairagya means "I want nothing" and "I am nothing." Sharanagati is "I am here for you, for your joy."

If you are grumbling, it is because these are lacking in your life. When you accept your situation you cannot grumble; when you take it as tapas you will not grumble. When you come from a state of dispassion – "I do not want anything" – you do not grumble; and if you are surrendered you will have no complaints.

All three of these – penance, dispassion and surrender – purify your mind and uplift you in joy.

If you do not do it willingly, you will do it out of desperation. First you will say, "Nothing can be done." Then in anger and desperation you will say, "I give up, I want nothing, I have no choice, to hell with it!"

Marseilles, France
May 28, 1997

*T*here is no problem that cannot be solved. When you have a problem that you think cannot be solved, you have accepted it. Then it is no longer a problem but a fact.

Suppose you think it is a problem that the ocean in Norway is too cold. Obviously, you cannot heat the ocean so it cannot be changed; you accept it and it is no longer a problem. Only when you are searching for a solution is there a problem. Thus there is no problem that cannot be solved. The moment you realize there is no solution, a problem ceases to be a problem.

The solution is the tail of every problem. Solutions come to you when you are calm and centered, when you use intelligence, when you are not lethargic but active, and when you have strong faith in divine law.

Oslo, Norway
February 3, 2000

*T*he "I" or ego in you is a tiny atom. If this atom is associated with the body, with matter, it identifies with matter. If this atom is associated with the being, the infinite, it identifies with the infinite. When this atom, this ego, identifies with the material world, it becomes mundane. When it identifies with the body, it becomes miserable. But when it is associated with the spirit, it becomes Divine. It becomes shakti – energy – when it is associated with the being, the Self.

In a huge atomic reactor, it is just one atom that is exploded. In the same way, in our whole body there is just one atom of "I." And when this "I" explodes, it becomes the light of the Self.

Usually we say "I am miserable," or "I am happy." Shift this atom of ego from identifying with the body and the conceptual world to identifying with the real world.

Montreal Ashram, Quebec, Canada
July 30, 1998

*W*hen you think well of yourself, in a very subtle way, you think badly about others. Then anger, jealousy and hatred follow. When you think badly about yourself, you feel low and again you become angry and you hate others. When you think well of yourself, you are in trouble and when you think badly of yourself, you are in greater trouble. So drop your self-image.

Mauritius
May 7, 1997

*E*go causes heaviness, discomfort. Ego does not let love flow. Ego can be transcended by knowing the truth, by inquiring "who am I?" Often, you feel contempt or jealousy towards someone who is egotistical. Instead you should have compassion or even pity.

There is also a positive aspect of ego. Ego drives you to do work. A person will do a job either out of compassion or out of ego. Most of the work in society is done out of ego. But in satsang, work is done out of love. Ego is separateness, non-belongingness. It desires to prove and to possess. When you wake up and see that there is nothing to be proven and nothing to possess, ego dissolves.

Bangalore Ashram, India
November 20, 1997

*T*here are three modes of communication: in head-to-head communication you talk, in heart-to-heart communication you sing, and soul-to-soul communication happens in silence.

When you meet with people, you often communicate from head-to-head. You keep talking, blabbering, and you keep communication only on the level of the intellect. When you are with nature, you start singing; you communicate with nature from your heart. And when you are with the guru, you go blank and forget all your questions. Then communication comes through the soul in silence.

When you meet with people, you prefer to remain in your head. Except when it is organized, you seldom sing with people. Your ego obstructs you from singing. When you sing with people, then you descend to the heart or feeling level. Some feel comfortable just listening to music. Some feel comfortable singing only when they are alone. Some sing to draw attention to themselves or to charm others. Some only want to join in when everyone else is singing. This type of singing all comes from ego.

Bhajan means sharing – sharing from the deepest level of our existence. Bhajan is authentic sharing. If you could truly sing with people, your ego would shatter. Children can sing with people for they do not have ego. To sing with a stranger you have to be free of ego.

The head level is safe for the ego. The heart level breaks the ego. The soul level dissolves the ego. The inability to communicate always happens because of ego.

Geilo, Norway
August 19, 1998

*J*ust as your car runs out of fuel and you have to refill it again and again, so your dedication and commitment run out over the course of time. They need constant renewal. You have to dedicate and rededicate again and again. Often people take their dedication for granted and then the mind starts demanding or complaining. When dedication is not complete, it leads to grumbling and complaints. Total dedication brings enormous enthusiasm, zeal, trust and challenge. Total dedication leaves no room for ego.

Vienna, Austria
May 21, 1997

*W*hat breaks intimacy?

- Taking a position, or ego
- Desires or expectations
- Insensitivity or too much sensitivity
- Judgments
- Taking intimacy for granted
- Finding imperfection in yourself or others
- Grumbling or lack of gratitude
- Lack of vivek – discretion, or lack of vairagya – dispassion

To maintain intimacy, dissolve into infinity. Dissolving into infinity brings you to the moment. Go beyond events and be in the moment. Dissolve into intimacy – this is the way to maintain it.

Bangalore Ashram, India
November 29, 1995

*N*either accept people as they are nor tolerate them.

Many people think tolerance is a virtue but tolerance is actually a negative term. If you like something, you do not have to tolerate it. Tolerance indicates a deep sense of dislike that can at any time turn into hatred. It indicates a sense of separateness, small mindedness, a limitation of consciousness.

When you tolerate, it is a temporary state. Tolerance is a potential volcano. If you are tolerating, it means you are just holding on. Acceptance is also negative. You accept that which is not lovable. Tolerance and acceptance come with judgment and separation.

Question: "But aren't we supposed to accept people as they are?"

If you do not love them, then you have to accept them. I tell you, do not accept people as they are. Just love them as they are.

Williams Island, Florida, United States
January 21, 1998

*T*hough you have often heard "do not judge," judgment comes unavoidably in day-to-day life. You either approve or disapprove of the actions and behaviors of people. But always remember that everything changes, so do not hold onto your judgment, otherwise your judgment becomes solidified like a rock, bringing misery for you and for others. If judgments are light as air, like a breeze, they bring in fragrance, and then move away. They can also bring a foul smell but then they also move away. Judgments should not stay forever. Judgments are so subtle that you are not even aware of their existence. Labeling someone as judgmental is also a judgment. Only in the state of Being, when you are full of love and compassion, can you ever be free from all judgments.

Yet the world cannot move without judgments. Until you judge something as good or bad, you cannot perform any actions. If you see rotten apples in the market, you refuse to buy them. You buy only good apples. If someone lies to you ten times, the next time they speak you think it could also be a lie. Such judgments happen automatically. But see the possibility that people and things can change at any time and do not hold onto your judgments.

Of course, you need to judge your company. Your company can pull you up or drag you down. The company that drags you towards doubt, dejection, blame, complaints, anger, delusion and desires is bad company. The company that pulls you up towards joy, enthusiasm, service, love, trust and knowledge is good company. When someone complains, first you listen, then you nod, then you sympathize, then you too complain. Just remember, do not let your judgments become permanent.

Montreal Ashram, Quebec, Canada
June 26, 1996

*I*n the company of your friend, you lose your centeredness. Your enemy puts you back in yourself. Your friend sympathizes with you and makes you believe in matter. Your enemy makes you feel helpless and takes you to the spirit. So your enemy is your friend and your friend is your enemy!

Krishna said to Arjuna, "One who is unfriendly everywhere – including to himself – his consciousness is stable and his awareness is established."

Rishikesh, India
March 19, 1997

*I*gnorance is being a skeptic and not knowing that you are one. If you think you are a skeptic, you can no longer be one because you have a clue of something beyond. So, in reality, you can never know if you are a skeptic or not! A skeptic is stuck in a paradigm, closing all other possibilities. But this creation is all possibilities. As one understands the paradigm shift, skepticism is removed.

A real scientist can never afford to be a skeptic because that closes down possibilities and does not allow him to probe into unknown areas of existence. Skepticism is an "I know it all" attitude, and such an attitude is unscientific. Perception and inference are two means of knowing and skepticism is dispelled by knowledge.

In every human being deep inside, there is faith and love. What you perceive as skepticism in someone is only a thin layer. If you hold in your mind that they are skeptics, you empower their skepticism. Do not acknowledge someone's skepticism by arguing with them because argument will only strengthen it. Fear of interference in one's freedom brings more resistance and causes skepticism. There is nothing better than your silence and a smile from your heart to dispel skepticism. Silence means the quality of consciousness, not just keeping your lips tight.

Skepticism does not arise in children. It comes only in people who walk within boundaries. Children live in their fantasy world, a world of many possibilities, a world of innocence, joy, beauty and so much love.

London, United Kingdom
November 1, 1995

*T*here are many ways to conquer the jealousy or envy that may arise in you –

* Know that the person of whom you are jealous or envious has done some good deeds in the past and is now reaping the fruit.

* See jealousy or envy as an inspiration to gain merit for yourself.

* Create a sense of belongingness with those of whom you are envious. See them as a part of you.

* Think of all you have that they do not have and feel grateful.

* Simply observe the sensations.

* Join hands and form a team with them.

* Realize that in the current of moving time all will perish – your envy along with what you envy.

And how do you handle jealousy in others?

* Think of everyone who is jealous of you for what you have and see that what they envy has not brought you joy.

* Praise them with superlatives.

* Create a sense of belongingness in them by your kind actions.

* Know that their feelings are temporary.

* It is best not to recognize their envy or jealousy at all. If you recognize a feeling as a reality, it only makes your ignorance grow.

* Know that all feelings and emotions are just passing clouds.

- ◆ Do not flaunt your talents to them.

- ◆ Know that they are puppets. They will all perish like apples and tomatoes – just with a longer shelf life.

- ◆ If nothing else works, just go to sleep.

European Ashram, Bad Antogast, Germany
August 4, 1999

*K*now that humiliation does not weaken you – it strengthens you. When you have a sense of belongingness, you cannot feel humiliated. The more egotistic you are, the more humiliation you feel. When you are childlike and have a greater sense of kinship, you do not feel humiliated. Similarly when you are committed to truth and not to your ego, you do not feel humiliated.

If you are afraid of humiliation, you can neither make progress in your material life nor in your spiritual life. When you stand above humiliation, you get closer to the Self – to God. When you are steeped in love, with existence, with the Divine, nothing whatsoever can humiliate you.

So the way out of humiliation is to get humiliated, be childlike, be crazy, get steeped in love with the Divine, and be totally committed to truth, to knowledge.

Montreal Ashram, Quebec, Canada
June 27, 2000

*W*hat do you do when someone behaves rudely to you?

- Get upset.
- Respond rudely.
- Become frustrated.
- Run away from the person or avoid the situation in the future.
- Blame the person.
- Preach to the person.

None of these will in any way strengthen you. What are the options? See someone's rude behavior in this light:

- Rudeness indicates the intensity of their commitment.
- It indicates their level of stress and insensitivity.
- It attests to the upbringing of the person.
- It indicates a persistent behavioral pattern.
- It shows a lack of knowledge.
- It shows a lack of insight into their own mind and its sensations.
- It shows you behavior to avoid.
- It is an opportunity for you to welcome and absorb the rudeness.
- It strengthens your mind.
- It renders unconditional the love that you are.

The next time someone is rude to you, make sure you do not get upset. Just return a broad smile. If you can digest rudeness, nothing whatsoever can shake you.

Thiruvananthapuram, Kerala, India
December 5, 1996

*D*o not let politics sway you away from the path. If you are afraid of politics you cannot be successful in the spiritual realm. You have to cross the barricade of politics. It is a test of your strength, your commitment and your focus.

You cannot avoid politics, but you choose whether to harbor the politics in your mind or to let it go. There was politics among the twelve apostles. There was politics among Buddha and his followers. Krishna was immersed in politics. And you say you do not want to get involved in politics? The more you do not want it, the more you will harbor it in your consciousness. When you recognize politics in any group, it is a blessing for you to be centered and to go inward. You can do that without blaming the group, without running away from people, without giving up. It can enhance your skill to act and to not get attached.

There are many advantages to becoming involved in politics. Politics amplifies the diversity in people. It confronts you with different viewpoints, approaches and tendencies. It enhances your ability to communicate and act. It brings centeredness and dispassion. It shakes you up and makes you stand up to the knowledge. It enhances your capacity to accept and tolerate. It makes you realize that all of life is a game.

Cross the threshold of politics and come to the Divine. The strong will smile through the politics and the weak will lament.

Paramaribo, Surinam
January 14, 1998

A dear person whom you trust lies to you and gets caught. What do you feel? Sadness, anger, resentment, disappointment, compassion, disillusionment, loss of respect, wonder, shock, embarrassment?

Recently when someone lied to me, I felt happy and more love, for he was not a good liar. Had he been a good liar, he would not have been caught. He was so innocent that he could not even lie properly. If he had not been caught, how would you know he was a liar? So you see, you can never know a good liar. The person you call a liar is not a good liar; he is innocent. So when someone lies to you, there is no need to react with sadness or disappointment. Instead just melt and dissolve in love.

Bangalore Ashram, India
September 6, 1995

W hy do you respect someone? You respect them because of good qualities such as honesty, wisdom, love and talents. But all these change in time and when they change, you lose respect. You only respect greatness.

I have tremendous respect for each and every one of you. Not for your greatness or wisdom or talent, but for the very person you are. I respect everyone totally, so I can never lose respect for anybody, however they may be. Someone does not need to be great in order to be respected. Respecting life makes you great. Do not look for respect from others – that makes you weak. Have respect for the Self and no one can take your self-respect.

Bangalore Ashram, India
February 29, 1996

*W*hen others respect you, it is not because you possess some virtues. It is because of their generosity, their greatness. If you say God is great, it makes you great. God is already great; your saying so does not affect God. When you respect someone, it only shows your own magnanimity. However many people you do not respect in the world, that much less is your wealth. If you respect everyone in the world, that much more is your value. Wise is the one who respects everyone.

Question: "But how can you respect a terrorist or a criminal?"

You should have respect for a terrorist because he shows you the way at his own cost. Respectfulness is a quality of refined consciousness. Respect for the Self is faith and faith is being open.

Bangalore Ashram, India
February 18, 1998

*R*espect everyone as you respect me, but do not expect from everyone what you expect from me.

You do it the other way. You do not respect everyone as you respect me, but you expect them to give you joy and you expect them to behave ideally. When they do not live up to your expectations, you get frustrated and you blame or curse them. By cursing, you lose your spiritual energy. Blessing raises your spiritual energy.

The world is full of differences; arguments are inevitable. With forbearance, patience and wisdom, skillfully make your way. If you find fools around you, they will make you wiser. The number of fools around you indicates the strength of your centeredness. Do not try to get rid of them!

If you are not centered, you will not have the patience to endure them. When you are totally established, you find that fools give you wisdom. They are your own reflection, there is no other. Fools offer you frustration or wisdom. The choice is yours.

European Ashram, Bad Antogast, Germany
July 17, 1996

*T*hank those who do not respect you. They have given you freedom. When people respect you, they often take away your freedom. They expect you to smile at them, recognize them and behave a certain way with them. If they do not respect you, you are not obliged to answer their questions and you can drop all formalities. You will be naturally smiling or frowning. Either way you will be complete.

When people love and respect you, you are obliged to return their courtesies because you do not want to hurt them. But when they do not respect or love you, they will not be hurt by your actions and words, so they set you free.

When you gain respect, you often do it at the cost of your freedom. Wisdom is to put freedom first and not bother with respect.

True freedom is not an "I don't care" attitude. It is lightness from within, a genuine smile and lack of stiffness. Such freedom will not bring arrogance. True love blossoms only in such freedom. And when there is genuine love, respect simply follows you.

European Ashram, Bad Antogast, Germany
July 30, 1997

*L*oyalty is the way in which a mature and integrated mind behaves. Loyalty signifies an undivided wholeness of consciousness and shows a richness of the mind. When the mind is not integrated it is feverish, disloyal and opportunistic.

Disloyalty comes out of opportunism which reveals a shortsightedness of one's destiny. Integrity or wholeness is essential to being healthy. A divided mind will gradually lead to schizophrenia and other mental and physical disorders. Loyalty is a real strength and will have the support of nature in the long run.

Fear and ambition are impediments to loyalty. Loyalty is needed both in the material and the spiritual plane. Loyalty is essential to destroy, create or maintain any institution, group or society.

Loyalty means believing in the continuity of commitment. Honoring commitment is loyalty. It takes you beyond the duality of craving and aversion.

Responsibility, dedication and commitment are the limbs of loyalty.

A loyal mind is a "yes"-mind. The purpose of asking questions is to get an answer. The purpose of all answers is to create a "yes." "Yes" is an acknowledgement of knowledge. The "yes"-mind is quiet, holistic and joyful. The "no"-mind is agitated, doubting and miserable. Loyalty begins with a "yes"-mind and starts to perish with a "no"-mind.

European Ashram, Bad Antogast, Germany
August 4, 1998

*O*ften when you praise, you praise in comparison to someone else. In order to praise one person, we put down someone else and when we want to point out someone's mistake, we praise another.

Some praise too little, and some are too shy to praise. Some are not accustomed to praising and just forget to do so. Some praise with motives, and some praise just to elevate. Others praise themselves in order to hide their low self-esteem. But real praise dawns in a blossomed state of consciousness.

The praise that comes out of an elevated state of consciousness simply arises from the nature of consciousness and is quite different. Normally praise comes out of craving and pride. Praise that comes from a heightened consciousness always comes out of fulfillment.

Praising can elevate the consciousness and bring enthusiasm and energy. But at the same time it can bring arrogance. Praising is a skill.

When someone praises you, do you take it without shying away? Accepting praise without shyness is also a skill.

En route to the Bangalore Railway Station, India
February 24, 2000

*W*hen do you appreciate someone? Don't you appreciate them when they do something that is unusual, not ordinary, something that is not their nature?

When a wicked person fails to cause problems, you appreciate them. Or when someone you think is not good performs a good deed, you appreciate them. When a good person does something extraordinary, you appreciate them. If a child makes you a cup of tea, you appreciate it, but if a mother made the same cup of tea, you are less likely to appreciate it because it is a normal act for her. In the same way, you appreciate getting a ride from someone you do not know, but you may not appreciate it from a bus driver.

In all these cases, the acts you praise are temporary, out of character, or not in the nature of that person. So when you appreciate someone for something, you imply that it is not the way they usually are.

Question: "What if a person wants to be appreciated?"

That means that the act is not in their nature, and that is why they want to be appreciated. If it is not coming from their nature, it is an imposed act.

So when you appreciate someone you imply that it is not their nature, that it is not the way they usually are. It is a rare act or quality. Appreciation implies a sense of separateness or distance, so watch out when you appreciate someone!

Vancouver, British Columbia, Canada
October 28, 1998

*T*o thank someone implies separation. Thanking means there are two. If you are deeply thankful, it means you deeply feel the separation. Deep within there is no need to thank because there is oneness. But you can thank superficially. Thanks are like ripples on the surface of the water.

When you say "thank you," you complete something. You are finishing a transaction, a relationship, a process. "Thank you" is like "goodbye." You can complete all transactions at a surface level, but deeper inside there is only oneness.

Thankfulness always exists in relation to something else. You do not thank for nothing at all, you thank for something. But in this case, something is less than nothing.

At the deepest level, thanking has no meaning. Does one hand thank the other hand? The deeper you go, you see there is no "other" to be thanked.

Seattle, Washington, United States
July 14, 1999

*T*oday is a gift from God – that is why it is called the present.

Are you grateful? If you are grateful, you do not belong to me. When someone gives you something, you are grateful; that means you feel separate. You are not grateful to yourself.

Gratefulness is inevitable but when you go beyond gratefulness, then union happens. No "I," no "you" remains. You are just one being with a thousand heads and a thousand arms, but with one heart.

You must be grateful on the path, but you have to transcend gratefulness. Small children do not feel grateful as long as they feel one. They take everything for granted. You are not grateful to your own hand that feeds you. It is better to stop being grateful.

When you are grateful then you are the center, you are more important. When you are grateful to God for having received something beautiful, for example, eyesight, who is important? You or God? You! Your gratitude indicates ego.

European Ashram, Bad Antogast, Germany
July 31, 1996

Question: "God is all abundant, all full and we are connected to God. Then why are we in debt? Why do some have and some do not?"

Is it only money that you are worried about? You have abundance, yet at the same time, you are indebted. How can both be true? How can you be indebted and at the same time have abundance? When you say you are indebted, that means you have received. Otherwise how can you be indebted? Be thankful for being indebted, because that means you have received. Those who have received should feel indebted. If you do not feel indebted, you cannot have abundance. So the more indebted you feel, the more abundance you have.

Feel indebted. Feel gratitude. Then abundance comes. As long as you crave abundance you get indebted. If you feel indebtedness and gratitude, then abundance comes.

Abundance and indebtedness coexist. You think you are indebted, but really you are not. It is better to feel totally indebted, because every bit of what you have, including your body, does not belong to you. Feel infinitely indebted for your body, for knowledge, for the things you have received, for your own life. Then you will bask in the abundance of the Creator.

Miami Beach, Florida, United States
February 8, 1996

*T*hose who are sensitive are often weak. Those who feel themselves strong are often insensitive. Some are sensitive to themselves but insensitive to others. Some are sensitive to others but not to themselves.

Those who are sensitive only to themselves often blame others. Those who are only sensitive to others often end up feeling self-pity. Some conclude it is better not to be sensitive at all because sensitivity brings pain, so they shut themselves off from others. But if you are not sensitive, you will lose all the finer things in life – intuition, love, joy.

This path and this knowledge make you both sensitive and strong. Often people who are insensitive do not recognize their insensitivity. And those who are sensitive often do not recognize their strength. Their sensitivity is their strength.

Sensitivity is intuition; sensitivity is compassion; sensitivity is love. Sensitivity is strength. Strength is calmness, endurance, silence, non-reactiveness, confidence, faith – and a smile.

Be both sensitive and strong.

Montreal Ashram, Quebec, Canada
June 18, 1997

*T*here are two types of compassion. One is the compassion of the wise; one is that of the ignorant.

An ignorant person's compassion is toward the fruit of an action – to alleviate the sickness or suffering that he witnesses. But a wise person's compassion is toward the lack of knowledge – to remedy the underlying reason for sickness or suffering.

Compassion for suffering shows ignorance. Suffering comes because of karma and if you believe in karma, where is compassion? You reap the fruit of your actions.

If a judge has compassion for offenders, then the jails will be empty. But are judges cruel to offenders? No. The judge's compassion is for the lack of knowledge he sees, not for the suffering of the criminals. It is the criminals' karma.

Often people think compassion is an act, an action. Know that compassion is your very nature. Then you will see that karma and compassion are not contradictory but rather complement one another.

Bangalore Ashram, India
September 15, 1999

*S*ome karma can be changed and some cannot.

When you prepare a dessert, if there is too little sugar or too little butter, too much or too little milk, it can all be adjusted, repaired. But once it is cooked, it cannot be reversed.

If buttermilk is sour, milk or salt can be added to make it drinkable but it can never be reversed back to milk.

Prabdha karma cannot be changed. Sanchita karma can be changed by spiritual practices. Satsang burns the seed of all negative karma.

When you praise someone, you take on their good karma.

When you blame someone, you take on their bad karma.

Know this and surrender both good and bad karma to the Divine and be free.

California, United States
June 29, 1995

*S*trange are the ways of karma. The more you understand it, the more amazed you become. Karma brings people together and separates them. It causes some to be weak and some to be strong. It makes some rich and some poor. All the struggles in the world, whatever they may be, are the bondage of karma. It cuts across all logic and reasoning. This understanding lifts you and keeps you from getting stuck in events or personalities and helps you in your journey to the Self.

Only human life has the ability to be free from karma. And only a few thousand aim to be free from it. Performing actions cannot eliminate karma. Only through grace can the bondage of karma be burnt.

Bangalore Ashram, India
April 24, 1996

*M*ercy indicates lack of intimacy – a distance, a lack of belonging. You do not have mercy on your loved ones. You do not hear parents say, "I have mercy on my children." You have mercy on those whom you think are not yours. Mercy implies the potential for anger, judgment and authority. When you ask for mercy, you are self-centered. You want to be excused from the law of cause and effect. It indicates lack of courage and valor.

At times, mercy is an impediment to growth. Mercy, of course, brings some comfort and relief, but it can impair the process of transformation. If the leaves were to ask for mercy from falling, they would not be transformed and what would happen to the tree?

You only ask for mercy when you have made a mistake and you think God is angry and is judging you. This is the small mind superimposing its nature on the Divine mind. The Divine is all knowing and all loving; there is no room for mercy. When you know and trust the process of creation, you will simply rejoice.

Do you know I have no mercy? When there is intimacy, there is no place for mercy.

Highway 25, Between Boulder and Denver, Colorado, United States
July 23, 1998

*W*hen there is so much love, you take total responsibility for any misunderstanding. For a moment you may express dismay on the surface. But when you do not feel that dismay in your heart, you arrive at a perfect understanding. You are in a state where all problems and all differences slide away and only love shines through.

Usually we are stuck in our differences because we have lost sight of ourselves. In the name of love we try to manipulate and control the other person. It is natural that when we love someone, we want them to be perfect.

You can never see the holes in the ground from the top of a hill. From an airplane the earth looks so smooth. So also from a state of elevated consciousness, you do not see the pitfalls in others. But if you come to the ground you always see the holes. When you want to fill the holes, you have to see them. You cannot build a home being airborne. You cannot till the land without looking at the holes, filling them, removing the pebbles.

That is why when you love someone, when you are close to them, you find faults in them. But finding faults destroys love and instead of helping to fill the holes, we run away. When you love someone and see their faults, stay with them and help them fill the holes. This is wisdom.

Bangalore Ashram, India
February 12, 1999

*W*hy do you love someone? Is it because of their qualities or because of a sense of kinship or intimacy?

You can love someone for their qualities and not feel a sense of kinship. This type of love gives rise to competition and jealousy. Such is not the case when love arises out of kinship.

If you love someone for their qualities, when the qualities change or you get accustomed to their qualities, your love also changes. However, if you love someone out of kinship, because they belong to you, then that love remains for lifetimes.

People say, "I love God because He is great." What if God is found to be ordinary, just one of us? Then your love for God would collapse. If you love God because He is yours, then however God is, whether He creates or destroys, you still love Him. The love of kinship is like the love for yourself.

Question: "Why do so many people have no love for themselves?"

No. It is just the opposite. They love themselves so much that they want better qualities for themselves. They want to appear better than they think they are. This love of qualities makes them hard on themselves.

If love is based on the qualities of a person, that love is not stable. After some time the qualities change and the love becomes shaky. Loving someone because of their greatness or uniqueness is third-rate love. Loving someone because they belong to you, great or otherwise, is unconditional love.

Knowledge, along with sadhana, seva and satsang – spiritual practice, service, and coming together in celebration – help to engender a sense of belonging. When love springs from a sense of belongingness, then the actions and qualities do not overshadow the love. Neither qualities nor actions can be perfect all the time. Only love and a feeling of kinship can be perfect.

European Ashram, Bad Antogast, Germany
August 12, 1998

*H*ere are the signs of love: When you love someone you see nothing wrong with them. Even if you see a fault in them you justify it in some way – "Everyone does that; it is normal." You think you have not done enough for them and the more you do, the more you want to do for them. They are always in your mind. Ordinary things become extraordinary. A baby winking at its grandmother becomes an extraordinary event. When you love someone, you want to see them always happy and you want them to have the best.

New Delhi, India
November 5, 1998

*T*here are some who long for change. Feeling that everything is stagnant in their lives, they want to change partners, careers, dwellings. There are some who are afraid of change. They feel security in the way they are.

There are some who see change, but do not acknowledge it out of fear. There are some who do not notice change at all. There are others who do not think there is anything to change.

There are some who realize that everything is changing, yet see there is something that is non-changing. Those who recognize the non-changing amidst the change are the wisest of all.

Question: "Must love always change?"

Love is your very nature. What is your nature cannot change. But the expression of love changes. Because love is your nature, you cannot but love.

The mother has total love for her child. Sometimes she feeds the child; sometimes she is strict with the child. "Come on, sit and write!" She does this out of love, and these are all different modes of love. So the expression of love changes. But love itself does not change, because love is your nature.

Montreal Ashram, Quebec, Canada
July 8, 1999

*W*hen someone expresses love to you, what do you do?

- You feel obliged and bound.
- You shrink or shy away.
- You feel foolish and awkward.
- You try to reciprocate even though it is not genuine.
- You doubt the love expressed and you doubt your own worthiness.
- You are afraid of losing respect because love does not allow distance and respect tends to keep a distance.
- Your ego hardens and does not allow you to receive and reciprocate.

The ability to receive genuine love comes with the ability to give love. The more you are centered and know by experience that you are love, the more you feel at home with any amount of love being expressed in any manner; for deep inside, you know love is not an emotion. It is your very existence.

Rishikesh, India
November 6, 1997

*J*oy is love for what is. Sorrow is love for what is not.

Rishikesh, India
April 3, 1997

*Y*ou feel love for someone and they do not accept it. What do you do?

- Get frustrated.
- Turn the love into hatred and wish for revenge.
- Again and again remind them how much you love them and how little they love you.
- Become fussy and cranky.
- Throw tantrums.
- Feel humiliated and try to protect your respect.
- Resolve never to love again.
- Feel hurt and mistreated.
- Try to be aloof and indifferent.

But you have seen that none of these work; they only make the situation worse. What is the way out of this? How do you maintain your lovingness?

- Have patience and change your expression of love.
- Be centered and limit your expression of love.
  Sometimes expressing love too much puts people off.
- Take it for granted that they love you too and just accept their style of expression.
- Genuinely acknowledge whatever love they have for you. This will turn your demand into gratefulness and the more grateful you are in life, the more love comes your way.
- Know that hurt is part of love and take responsibility for it. When you move away from your center, you will get hurt and the nature of worldliness is misery.

Jaipur, Pink City, India
November 13, 1997

*B*eing in utter love inspires. It brings confidence in applying knowledge. The visible sign of utter love is an undying smile.

Bangalore Ashram, India
November 11, 1999

*L*et love be. Do not give it a name. When you give love a name it becomes a relationship, and relationships restrict love.

There is love between you and me. Just let it be. If you give love a name, such as brother, sister, mother, father, guru – you are making it into a relationship. Imposing a relationship on love restricts it. What is your relationship to yourself? Are you your wife, brother, husband, guru? Let love be. Do not give it a name.

Topanga Canyon, California
July 16, 1997

*W*hen love glows, it is bliss.
When it flows, it is compassion.
When it blows, it is anger.
When it ferments, it is jealousy.
When it is all "no's", it is hatred.
When it acts, it is perfection.
When love knows, it is me.

Bangalore Ashram, India
September 17, 1997

*W*ith whom do you feel really comfortable and at ease?
You feel comfortable with someone who does not question
your love, someone who takes for granted that you love them.
If someone doubts your love and you constantly have to prove
it, this becomes a heavy burden for you. When someone doubts
your love, they start questioning you and demanding
explanations for all your actions. Explaining everything you do
is a burden. Your nature is to shed burdens, so when your love
is questioned, you do not feel comfortable.

When you question the reason behind an action, you are asking
for justice for yourself and you create a distance. Your whole
intention is to come close, but by asking for justice you create a
distance. When someone asks for an explanation, they are
speaking from doership and are imposing that doership on you.
This brings discomfort.

If someone is just there with you, a part of you, they do not
question you. They are like your arm. There is a thorough
understanding and questions do not arise. Neither demand an
explanation nor give an explanation.

You are a witness to all your actions. You are as much a
stranger to your own actions as you are to someone else's
actions. You are the eternal witness.

Montreal Ashram, Quebec, Canada
July 9, 1997

*O*nly one who has renounced can truly love. To the degree you have renounced, to that degree will you have the ability to love. Often people think those who renounce cannot love, and those who love cannot renounce. This is because renunciates do not seem to be in love, and so-called lovers are possessive and needy.

True love is not possessive; it brings freedom, and renunciation is nothing but freedom. Only in freedom can love blossom fully. When you are in love you say, "I want nothing; I just want this." Renunciation is, "I do not want anything. I am free." In love there are no other needs. Renunciation is having no need. Love and renunciation, although appearing to be opposites, are two sides of the same coin.

Only renunciation can sustain love and joy. Without renunciation love turns into misery, possessiveness, jealousy and anger. Renunciation brings contentment and contentment sustains love. Without renunciation one gets discontented, frustrated, sad, fearful, suspicious, analytical. And the whole soap opera begins.

So-called renunciates have run away from life frustrated and disappointed. Real renunciation is born out of knowledge and wisdom – knowledge of life in the background of time and space and in the context of this magnanimous universe.

Montreal Ashram, Quebec, Canada
June 30, 1999

*Y*ou have to rejoice in the means. You have to love the means. Love is the goal but the means must also be lovable. Love springs forth when there is no effort, when all activities are shunned.

Montreal Ashram, Quebec, Canada
October 14, 1998

*L*ove is your nature. In the process of its expression, you often become ensnared in the object. This is when your sight is caught outside. To return to your nature, you need insight.

Pain is the first insight. It takes you away from the object and turns you towards your body and mind.

Energy is the second insight. A bolt of energy brings you back to your Self.

Divine love is the third insight. A glimpse of Divine love makes you complete and overrules all relative pleasures.

Trance is the fourth insight. An elevation of consciousness and partial awareness of the physical reality around you is trance. This brings you back to your nature.

Realization of non-dual existence – that everything is made up of one and only one – is the fifth insight.

Bangalore Ashram, India
September 17, 1997

*I*n love you elevate an object to life. When you love an object, it becomes alive.

For children everything is personal. Children take each object and make it totally personal. Even a stone has a face; even the sun laughs. When you attach emotion to it, all of creation becomes personal. When you remove emotion, even people become objects. Violence is removing emotion. How can a person kill another human being? Violence only happens when someone does not see the other person as a human being; they see them as an object. But even a stone attracts reverence when it becomes personal.

In military training soldiers are taught to see people as deadly objects coming toward them that need to be killed first. But in a temple even a stone is elevated to the level of spirit.

The impersonal cannot attract reverence. Most people see God as impersonal and therefore they do not progress. When we say something is not real, then it is impersonal. When we personalize something, we make it real. So then, what is reality? You are the reality. You are not your thoughts; you are not your emotions nor your actions. You are not even just a person — you are the reality.

Montreal Ashram, Quebec, Canada
June 25, 1997

*T*here are three kinds of love: the love that comes out of charm, the love that comes out of comfort, and Divine love.

The love that comes out of charm does not last long. It comes out of unfamiliarity or out of attraction. In this love, you lose attraction quickly, and boredom sets in, like most love marriages. This love may diminish and bring along with it fear, uncertainty, insecurity and sadness.

The love that comes out of comfort and familiarity grows. You are more comfortable with an old friend who is a familiar person, rather than with a new person. But this love has no thrill, no enthusiasm, no joy or fire in it.

Divine love supersedes all other love. Divine love is always new and the closer you get, the more charm and depth you experience. Divine love brings comfort, familiarity and enthusiasm. There is never boredom and it keeps you alert and aware.

Worldly love can be like an ocean, yet an ocean has a bottom. Divine love is like the sky – limitless, infinite. From the bottom of the ocean, soar into the vast sky.

Bangalore Ashram, India
April 24, 1997

*B*eyond an event is knowledge. Beyond a person is love. Beyond an object is infinity.

Knowledge is not in an event; it is beyond events. If you take one event and infer anything from it – infer knowledge – it will be erroneous knowledge. If someone gets angry and shouts, you attribute anger to that person, but actually the anger was carried from someone else to her. Someone else got angry first and someone before that and someone else before that and on and on.

When you go beyond an event, only then will truth dawn. One particular event gives you a false notion, so you have to consider the totality of events, the totality of all events infinitely. Beyond the event is knowledge.

What do we call a person? A person is a body, a mind, a complex of behaviors that is changing. Love is unchanging. Beyond the person is love. When you lose your personality, you become love. If you cannot lose yourself, you cannot find yourself. So, lose your personality and find yourself.

Behind every object is infinity. An object is limited. Reduce an object to atoms and you will find that each atom contains infinite space. Beyond the object is infinity.

Maya – delusion – is getting caught up in the event, in the personality, in the object. Knowledge, love, Brahman – divine consciousness – is seeing beyond all these. Do you see? This is just a little shift. The object behind the object is infinity. The person behind the person is love.

Big Sur, California, United States
June 21, 1995

85

*T*here are five aspects to your Self:

- Asti – is-ness
- Bhaati – knowledge or expression
- Preeti – love
- Nama – name
- Rupa – form

Matter has two aspects: nama and rupa – name and form. Consciousness has three aspects: asti – it is; bhaati – it knows and expresses; and preeti – it is loving. This is the secret of the whole universe. Maya – ignorance or delusion – is not being aware of the three aspects of consciousness and getting caught up in name and form.

Question: "Why are we imperfect?"

So that we can grow to perfection. Life is a movement from imperfection to perfection. A seed contains the tree but to become a tree it must cease being a seed. The seed is not a tree. A sapling is not a tree. So in life you can either see imperfection at every step, or you can see movement from one perfection to another.

Wherever you put your attention, that will grow. If you put your attention on the lack of something, the lack will increase.

Bangalore Ashram, India
December 19, 1996

*H*ow can you always be happy? Forget about "always" – then you will be happy.

In always wanting to be comfortable, you become lazy.
In always wanting perfection, you become angry.
In always wanting to be rich, you become greedy.

Fear arises when we do not realize that only life is for always. This projection of the nature of self – which is "always" – onto the temporal – which can never be "always" – is called maya.

Bangalore Ashram, India
November 4, 1999

*W*hen something is unbelievably beautiful or joyful, you wonder if it is a dream. Often what you perceive as reality is not joyful so when misery is there, you never wonder if it is a dream. You are sure it is real. This is knowing the real as unreal and unreal as real. In fact, all the miseries are unreal. A wise man knows that happiness is real, as it is your very nature. Unhappiness is unreal because it is inflicted by memory. When you see everything as a dream, then you abide in your true nature.

A nightmare is a dream mistaken for reality. There is no confusion in a dream at all. Keep wondering whether all this is a dream and you will wake up to the real.

Lake side, Chandigarh, India
March 26, 1998

*I*llusion is an error of perception and knowing illusion as illusion is knowledge. Our experience of the world is based on perception. Since every perception is erroneous, the world is an illusion. Experiences are based on perception. The one who experiences is the only reality. Look for the seer, the one who experiences, in between the experiences. Every experience leaves a residue that clouds the intellect. Wake up this moment. Shake your head of all past experiences and look at the pure Being that I am and that you are.

Question: "How do you distinguish the experience from the one who experiences?"

Are you really here? Are you listening? Now close your eyes and see who is listening, who is questioning, who is sitting, and who wants what. Who is confused? This is the one who experiences.

Bangalore Ashram, India
May 9, 1996

*W*hat is vivek? Vivek means knowing that everything is changing. Time and again you have to awaken to this – the world, the people, our body, our emotions, are constantly changing. When you experience sorrow, understand that vivek has been overshadowed.

Jakarta, Indonesia
April 10, 1996

*Y*ou can be at ease with the uncertainty of the world when you realize the certainty of consciousness. Often people do just the opposite. They are certain about the world and uncertain about God. They rely on something that is not reliable and get upset. Uncertainty causes craving for stability, yet the most stable thing in the universe is our Self.

The world is of change; the Self is of non-change. You have to rely on the non-change and accept the change. If you are certain that everything is uncertain, then you are liberated. When you are uncertain in ignorance, then you become worried and tense. Uncertainty with awareness brings higher states of consciousness and a smile.

Often people think that certainty is freedom. If you feel freedom when you are not certain, that is real freedom. Often your certainty or uncertainty is based on the relative world. Being certain about the uncertainty of the relative makes you certain about the existence of the absolute and brings a certain faith in the absolute.

Question: "Can we still be enthusiastic when we are uncertain?"

Yes. In knowledge you can be enthusiastic in uncertainty. Often people who are uncertain do not act; they simply sit and wait. Acting in uncertainty makes life a game, a challenge. Being in uncertainty is letting go. Certainty about the relative world creates dullness. Uncertainty about the Self creates fear. Uncertainty about matter brings certainty about consciousness.

Bangalore Ashram, India
December 10, 1997

*W*hen you feel time is too short, you are either restless or in expanded awareness. When you feel time is too long, you are miserable or keen-minded. When you are happy and love what you are doing, you simply do not feel the time. Similarly, in sleep you do not feel time.

When you are ahead of time, it drags and is boring. When time is ahead of you, then you are surprised and shocked. You cannot digest events.

In deep meditation, you are time and everything is happening in you. Events are happening in you like the clouds that come and go in the sky.

When you are with time, you are wise and at peace.

Bangalore Ashram, India
April 8, 1999

*W*hen the mind is happy, it expands; then time feels too short. When the mind is unhappy, it contracts; then time feels too long. When the mind is in equanimity, it transcends time.

To escape from the two extremes, many resort to alcohol or sleep but when the mind is dull or unconscious, it is unable to experience itself. Samadhi – no-mindedness or timelessness – is peace, the real peace. That is the greatest healer.

Just as the mind experiences time, this moment has a mind of its own, a Big Mind with enormous and infinite organizing power. Thought is nothing but a ripple in this moment, and a few moments of samadhi infuse the mind with energy.

Before you fall into slumber or as soon as you wake up from sleep, in the moments of twilight of consciousness, experience the timelessness.

Bangalore Ashram, India
December 10, 1997

*L*ife is a combination of form and formless. Feelings have no form but their expressions have form. The Self has no form but its abode has form.

Similarly, wisdom and grace have no form but are expressed through form. Discarding the formless, you become inert, materialistic and paranoid. Discarding the form, you become a dreamer, a lost ascetic, or emotionally unbalanced.

Vanprastha Ashram, Rishikesh, India
March 9, 2000

*T*he Divine can come only in deep rest, not in doing. All your activities help you to become silent, and not enjoying bliss and peace can take you even further. If existence wants to give you these – fine. Accept them. But enjoying bliss and peace can cause cravings. It takes courage to say, "I am." Your true nature is bliss but when you try to enjoy the bliss, you step down from "I am" to "I am peaceful," "I am blissful." And that is followed by "I am miserable."

"I am" is dispassion. Dispassion welcomes everything. Centeredness brings energy, a spark. But enjoying bliss brings inertia. If you are dispassionate, the bliss is still there. Dispassion takes away the sense of scarcity. Passion is a sense of lacking abundance. When everything is abundant, dispassion happens and when dispassion is there, everything comes in abundance.

Lake Tahoe, California, United States
July 15, 1998

*A*ctivity and rest are two vital aspects of life. To find a balance in them is a skill in itself. Wisdom is knowing when to have rest, when to have activity, and how much of each to have. Finding them in each other – activity in rest and rest in activity – is the ultimate freedom.

More tiring than the work itself is the memory of hard work. Just thinking you have worked hard interferes with the quality of rest. Some people take pride in working hard without any results. And there are others who crave for a long rest without knowing that true rest is in non-doership.

Thinking you need rest makes you restless.
Thinking you have to work hard makes you tired.
Thinking you have worked hard brings self-pity.

It is the quality of rest, even if it is short, that helps you to recuperate. When rest is needed, your body will automatically take it. Resting, without thinking about the need for it, is more restful. Lack of desire, dispassion and samadhi are the deepest forms of rest.

Bangalore Ashram, India
September 10, 1998

*H*ide your dispassion and express your love. Expressing dispassion may bring ego. By expressing dispassion you lose enthusiasm in life and by not expressing love you feel stifled. Hide dispassion in your heart like the roots of a tree and express love like a ripe fruit.

Halifax, Nova Scotia, Canada
June 22, 2000

*W*hen you are in the grip of feverishness over the results of your actions, what should you do?

Have faith and confidence that the results will be much better than you can ever imagine. With faith you can rid yourself of the feverishness of action and achievement. Feverishness can be a residue from over-activity. Sleeping, listening to flute music and bathing in cold water can help.

When you are doing something very important, take a moment to do something totally unrelated, irrelevant and insignificant. This enhances your creativity. Relevant action keeps you bound to the action. Irrelevant action makes life a game.

Have dispassion. Know that everything passes one way or the other, and that it does not matter. Meditation and breathing can calm you down.

Delhi, India
March 29, 2000

*F*alse securities do not allow your faith to grow. When you drop your securities, your faith will grow. When you buffer your life with securities, you keep faith away. It is faith that brings perfection in you. Faith is the greatest security.

If you have material securities and do not have faith, you will still reel in fear. You must let go of all possessions in the mind. False security is keeping things where they do not belong. Having a job, a house, friends – these are all illusions of security.

Keep the house where it belongs, not in the mind. Keep the money in the bank or in the pocket, not in the mind. Keep friends and family where they belong, not in the mind.

The Divine is your only security. Faith is realizing that you always get what you need. Faith is giving the Divine a chance to act. Your body belongs to the world. Your spirit belongs to the Divine.

Santa Monica, California, United States
January 28, 1998

*H*ave faith in sound and then move on to have faith in silence. Have faith in sound when it is pleasant and have faith in silence when sound is unpleasant.

People seem to have more faith in chatting and gossip rather than in chanting and knowledge. When someone says something negative, you immediately believe it and your mind becomes more disturbed. Believing in an unpleasant sound creates turmoil in your mind. When this happens, shift your faith to silence.

Have faith in sound like the chanting of mantras. Have faith in knowledge. Have faith in silence.

Bangalore Ashram, India
October 28, 1999

*F*aith is the subject of the head; devotion is the subject of the heart; meditation is the subject of the head and the heart, and connects them both.

A mature intellect is devoted; a mature heart is full of knowledge; and meditation matures your intellect as well as your heart. The intellect puts more faith in matter and the heart puts more faith in the abstract.

It is nearly impossible for you to be in total lack of faith or total lack of devotion. It is only a question of balance. All of your life becomes a meditation. Whether you look at the trees or the flowers or talk with people, you are in meditation.

Los Angeles, California, United States
August 7, 1996

*I*n science knowledge comes first and then faith follows. In spirituality faith comes first and then knowledge follows.

The knowledge that pesticides and chemical fertilizers are good for plants came through science. Based on this knowledge, people had faith in pesticides and fertilizers and they were used all over the world. Then a different knowledge came and faith shifted to organic farming. Knowledge brought faith, the knowledge changed, and then faith changed. The knowledge and faith of science is of "happening."

In spirituality, faith is first and knowledge comes later. Just as in Sudarshan Kriya, yoga and meditation – first you have faith and then knowledge follows. If you do pranayama faithfully, then you get the knowledge of the prana – life energy. If you do your meditation faithfully, the knowledge of consciousness follows. Even an illiterate person, through faith, attains deep knowledge.

Science regards life as matter and spirituality regards matter as life. Science sees even human beings as matter, and spirituality considers even the earth to be a mother; even rivers and mountains become living beings.

Oslo, Norway
February 21, 1996

*I*f you think your faith in God does God a favor, you are mistaken. Your faith in God or your guru does nothing for God or guru. Faith is your wealth.

Faith gives you strength instantly. Faith brings you stability, centeredness, calmness and love. Faith is your blessing. But here is a paradox: If you lack faith, you have to pray for faith. Yet to pray, you need faith.

People put their faith in the world, but the whole world is just a soap bubble. People have faith in themselves, but they do not know who they are. People think they have faith in God, but they do not really know who God is.

There are three types of faith:

♦ Faith in yourself – Without faith in yourself, you think, "I cannot do this. This is not for me. I will never find freedom in this life."

♦ Faith in the world – You must have faith in the world or you cannot move an inch. You deposit money in the bank with the faith that it will be returned. If you doubt everything, nothing will work for you.

♦ Faith in the Divine – Have faith in the Divine and you will evolve.

All these faiths are connected. You must have all three for each to be strong. If you start doubting one, you will begin to doubt everything.

Atheists seem to have faith in themselves and faith in the world but not in God. Yet they do not actually have complete faith in themselves. And their faith in the world cannot be constant because the world is always changing. Lack of faith in God, the world or yourself brings fear. Faith makes you full – faithful.

Having faith in the world without having faith in God does not bring complete peace. If you have faith and love, you automatically have peace and freedom. People who are extremely disturbed should only have faith in God to help overcome their problems.

There is a difference between faith and confidence. Faith is the beginning. Confidence is the result. Faith in yourself brings freedom. Faith in the world brings you peace of mind. Faith in God evokes love in you.

Bangalore Ashram, India
May 28, 1998

*I*f you have no faith there is no point in asking any questions because how can there be any faith in the answer you receive? But if you have complete faith, then there are no questions.

If you have faith in God or in yourself or in your family and friends, then questions cannot arise. When you know someone is taking care of you, what is the need for questions? If you have taken the Karnataka Express to Bangalore, there is no need to ask at every station, "Where is the train going?" When someone is taking care of your desires, why go to an astrologer?

Mumbai, India
September 3, 1997

*F*aith is the nature of an undivided mind, an undivided consciousness. You have faith in God so do not try to know God. You have faith in the Self so do not try to know the Self. Do not try to make into an object of knowing anything in which you have faith. The child has faith in her mother. She does not try to know her mother; she simply has faith in her mother. When you have faith, what is the need to know? If you try to make love an object of knowing, it will disappear. God, love, Self and sleep are all beyond knowing.

If you try to analyze, doubts arise and faith will disappear. So do not attempt to know or analyze anything in which you want to have faith. Analysis creates a distance; synthesis brings things together. Faith is synthesis; knowing is analysis.

Faith and belief are different. Beliefs are diluted; faith is stronger, more concrete. Our beliefs can change but faith is firm.

Consciousness cannot exist without faith. It is like the flame of a candle. Faith is a relaxed, stable quality of consciousness. Faith is the nature of consciousness.

European Ashram, Bad Antogast, Germany
May 27, 1999

*T*ruth is that which does not change. Examine your life and identify all that changes as "not truth." With this outlook, you will find that you are surrounded by only untruth.

When you identify untruth, then you will become free from it. When you do not identify the untruth, you cannot become free from it. Your own experiences in life make you identify your own untruth.

As you mature in life, you find everything is untruth – events, situations, people, emotions, thoughts, opinions, concepts, your body – everything is untruth. It is only then that satsang – the company of truth – happens in the real sense. A mother cannot see the child as untruth until the child becomes an adult. For a baby, sweetness is not untruth, and for a teenager, sex is not untruth.

Knowledge is untruth if it is only words. But as existence, it is truth. Love as an emotion is not truth; as existence, it is truth.

European Ashram, Bad Antogast, Germany
June 15, 2000

*W*hen we are joyful, we do not look for perfection. If you are looking for perfection then you are not at the source of joy. Joy is the realization that there is no vacation from wisdom. The world appears imperfect on the surface but underneath, all is perfect. Perfection hides; imperfection flaunts itself.

The wise will not stay on the surface but will probe into the depths. The things you see are not blurred; it is your vision that is blurred. Infinite actions prevail in the wholeness of consciousness, and yet consciousness remains perfect, untouched. Realize this now and be at home.

Somewhere in British Columbia, Canada
June 19, 1996

*L*egendary is the love that withstands rejection. It will be free of anger and ego.

Legendary is the commitment that withstands humiliation. It will be one-pointed and will reach the goal.

Legendary is the wisdom that withstands turbulence. It will be integrated into life.

Legendary is the faith that withstands a million chances of doubt. It will bring perfection – siddhis.

Legendary are the events that withstand time. They will become morals for the millions.

Montreal Ashram, Quebec, Canada
July 5, 2000

CHAPTER TWO

The Path to the Goal That is You

A poor man celebrates the New Year once a year. A rich man celebrates each day. But the richest man celebrates every moment.

How rich are you? Do you celebrate once a year? Once a month? Every day? If you celebrate every moment, you are the Lord of Creation.

Review the year while you celebrate. This is your homework. What did you do? What did you achieve? How useful were you this past year? Sit for an hour and think about every week, one minute per week, and see the year's growth in less than an hour. With a flower, on New Year's Day, offer the whole year to the Divine.

Weggis, Switzerland
December 27, 1995

*H*uman life is a combination of matter, or body, and spirit, or vibration. Joy is becoming intense vibration and forgetting that you are matter.

Carnal instincts can make you momentarily feel intense vibrations. That is how they give you a glimpse of joy. But such joy is short-lived, eventually making you dense.

Pleasure that comes from satsang is of a higher nature. Mantras and singing create vibrations in the spirit. That is why when you meditate and sing, ecstasy continues for a long time.

Pleasure in the subtle is long-lasting, energizing, refreshing and freeing. Pleasure from the gross is short-lived, tiring and binding.

When you know you are electricity – vibration or energy – then craving, greed, lust and anger disappear and you become true celebration.

European Ashram, Bad Antogast, Germany
December 24, 1997

*L*et time celebrate your presence. People usually make a wish for the New Year, but this year, make no wish. Let the New Year celebrate you. If the New Year wants to bring you nicer things, just let it.

Usually you are lost in celebration. When you let time celebrate you, you are a witness amidst celebration.

The New Year is fortunate because you are living at this time. When you are living for the sake of the world, the world is fortunate. You are not living for yourself, but for the world. Whatever the world needs or wants, you are here for that.

Lake Lucerne, Switzerland
January 1, 1997

*W*hen you feel you are stuck in life and not growing, or are bombarded by desires, when you feel dryness, no enthusiasm, no juice, what do you do?

Here is the solution: feel generous – right now, not tomorrow, but right now.

Both a princess and a pauper can feel generous. Generosity is a quality of the spirit. When you feel generous, your life becomes abundant – full of compassion and love.

Question: "Is generosity the same as gratitude?"

No. Gratitude always has self-concern. You are grateful because you have something or you get something. Generosity is an expression that is independent of external circumstances. No one can make you feel generous. That is something that you must do yourself. Essentially generosity is not an act. It is a state of consciousness, but it always finds its expression in an act.

Question: "What about passion?"

Passion indicates scarcity. Dispassion is abundance. Dispassion without generosity makes you self-centered and causes more dryness.

Thinking about our past generosity only brings doership. Drop that and just feel generous.

Vancouver, British Columbia, Canada
July 1, 1998

*O*ur first and foremost commitment in the world is to do seva, or service.

If there is fear or confusion in your life, it is because you lack commitment. The very thought, "I am here in this world to do seva," dissolves the "i" and when the "i" dissolves, worries dissolve. Seva is not something you do out of convenience or for pleasure. The ultimate purpose of life is to be of service.

An uncommitted mind is miserable. A committed mind may at times experience rough weather but it will reap the fruits of its toil.

When you make service your sole purpose in life, it eliminates fear, focuses your mind and gives you meaning.

Bangalore Ashram, India
November 12, 1998

*P*oor people fight for food. Rich people share their food. Richer are those who share power. Richer still are those who share fame. Richest of all are those who share themselves. A person's wealth is measured by his ability to share and not by what he hoards.

Bangalore Ashram, India
October 24, 1996

*W*hat does success mean? There is no question of success if you have nothing to gain. There is nothing to gain if you have come only to give and serve. Success implies non-supremacy. It indicates that there is a chance of failure. If something is supreme, there is nothing to lose.

Success means going beyond a limit. To exceed a limit you need to assume that you have a limit. Assuming a limit is underestimating yourself. If you have no boundaries, then where is your success? You do not say that you successfully drank a glass of water, because it is well within your capabilities. But when you do something that is beyond your perceived limits, you claim success.

When you realize your unboundedness, then no action is an achievement.

Anyone who runs after success or who claims to be successful only reveals his limitation. If you feel very successful, it means that you have underestimated yourself. All your achievements can only be smaller than you. Taking pride in any achievement is belittling yourself.

Question: "What if you feel that you are not serving successfully?"

When you serve others, you may feel that you have not done enough but you will never feel that you have been unsuccessful. Real service is when you feel that you have not done enough.

Oslo, Norway
June 2, 1999

*W*ork does not tire you as much as does the sense of doership. All of your talents are for others. If you have a good voice, it is for others to hear. If you are a good cook, it is so others may eat. If you write a book, it is so others can read it. If you are a good carpenter, it is to build things for others to use. If you are a good surgeon, it is to heal others. If you are a good teacher, it is so others may learn. All of your work and talents are for others. If you do not make use of your talents, they will not be given to you again.

European Ashram, Bad Antogast, Germany
July 24, 1996

*W*hen you do seva, you are not doing others a favor. After doing seva you are rewarded immediately. The reward of seva is certain and is always more than your doing. Expecting a reward for seva turns the seva into labor.

If you think you have done much, you will do very little; if you see you have done little, then you will do more.

Labor means that even after a reward, there will be complaints. In seva there is no complaint, even when you see no immediate reward. Be grateful for any opportunity to do seva.

Maui, Hawaii, United States
February 19, 1997

*T*he first sign of intelligence is not to begin anything – not to be born at all.

Failing this, the second sign of intelligence is, once you have started something, to see it through to the end. Shortsighted people look for short-term benefits. Far-sighted people look for long-term benefits.

Whether you consider yourself intelligent or not, there is no escape from seva. Seva gives you immediate satisfaction as well as long-term merits.

Rishikesh, India
March 18, 1999

*T*he more you give, the more strength will be given to you.

Bangalore Ashram, India
September 24, 1997

*T*he way to expand from individual to universal consciousness is to share the sorrow and joy of others. As you grow, your consciousness should also grow. As you expand in knowledge over time, depression is not possible. Your innermost source is joy.

The way to overcome personal misery is to share universal misery. The way to expand personal joy is to share universal joy. Instead of thinking, "What about me?" "What can I gain from this world?" think, "What can I do for the world?" When everyone considers only what they can contribute to society, you will have a divine society. We have to educate and culture our individual consciousness to expand over time with knowledge – to change from "What about me?" to "What can I contribute?"

If you are not having good experiences in meditation, then do more seva – you will gain merit and your meditation will be deeper. When you bring some relief or freedom to someone through seva, good vibrations and blessings come to you. Seva brings merit; merit allows you to go deep in meditation and meditation brings back your smile.

St. Louis, Missouri, United States
June 13, 1996

*M*any people stop doing seva when they put their self-image, their prestige, their need for respect, their comfort and convenience above their goal. What is more important to you?

People shy away from seva when they do not receive a good position or when they get insulted. People stop doing seva when they feel they are not getting what they expected. They stop their seva when working towards their goal becomes a struggle rather than a challenge. As a result only a few people in the world succeed in reaching their true goal.

Bangalore Ashram, India
September 1, 1999

*S*ervice without attitude
Love without reason
Knowledge without intellect
Life beyond time and events
is what you are.

Bangalore Ashram, India
May 16, 1996

*Y*ou cannot rest when you have to do something that you cannot do. And you cannot rest when you feel you have to be someone whom you are not. You are not required to do what you cannot. You will not be asked to give more than you can give. Nothing is expected of you that you cannot do. Doing service involves only doing what you can do; no one wants you to be someone you are not.

This realization brings you deep rest. You cannot rest if you are ambitious or lethargic. Both are opposed to good rest. A lazy person will toss and turn at night and be "rest-less" and an ambitious person will burn inside.

Deep rest cultures your talents and abilities and brings you closer to your nature. Even a slight feeling that the Divine is with you will give you deep rest. Prayer, love and meditation are all flavors of deep rest.

Boston, Massachusetts, United States
May 6, 1999

*S*acrifice is letting go of something that you are holding on to or that you are attached to – giving up something that gives you pleasure for something bigger that can bring good. Sacrifice brings strength in life. Life without sacrifice is stagnant. Sacrifice is a quantum leap; it takes you to a higher level.

Often people think sacrifice makes life dull and joyless. In fact, it is sacrifice that makes life worth living. Sacrifice cultures your magnanimity and helps you move beyond misery. A life without sacrifice is worth nothing. Zeal, enthusiasm, strength and joy all come from sacrifice.

Some people complain, "I have sacrificed so much." But that is good. The thought of sacrifice has given them the strength to complain and saves them from blaming themselves. Without this they would be even more depressed.

Sacrifice never goes unrewarded. There can be no love, no wisdom and no true joy without sacrifice. Sacrifice makes you sacred. Become sacred.

European Ashram, Bad Antogast, Germany
August 6, 1997

*A*usterity is often mistaken for poverty or self-denial. It is neither. Austerity comes out of maturity. It is a sign of social health.

People who practice austerity are often resentful of richness. This is a pitiable state. Such austerity is not born out of maturity but out of compulsion. True austerity has tolerance for richness and is never resentful. In fact, one who is mature will have pity for one who is not austere.

Vanity is poverty of the spirit and austerity brings freedom from the pride of vanity. But taking pride in austerity is also vanity. Austerity is not opposed to celebration and vanity alone cannot be celebration. Celebration dawns in the spirit. Only one who is rich in spirit can practice austerity. One may be rich materially but if he is poor in spirit, he can neither celebrate nor evolve.

Austerity comes out of abundance, and austerity brings abundance. If you feel a lack in any area of life, immediately start austerity. Austerity not only brings freedom but nurtures sharing and caring.

Bangalore Ashram, India
November 19, 1998

*L*ife is utterly simple and yet most complex. You have to simultaneously attend to both facets of life. When life appears most complex, turn to simplicity. Simplicity brings peace. When you are peaceful attend to the complexity within you. That will make you more skillful.

If you are only with simplicity, it makes you lazy and dull. Being only with complexity makes you angry and frustrated. The intelligent ones balance them and rejoice in both. If you look only to simplicity, growth is not there. If you look only at the complexity, there is no life at all. All that you need is a skillful balance. If you recognize both the simplicity and the complexity of life, you will be skillfully peaceful.

Colors are the complexity of life. White is the simplicity. When your heart is pure, your life becomes colorful.

Rishikesh Ashram, India
March 26, 1997

*Y*our life is a gift and you have come to unwrap the gift. In the process of unwrapping, remember to also save the wrapper.

Your environment, the situations around you, the circumstances in which you find yourself, and your body are the wrapping paper. When we unwrap, we often destroy the wrapping paper. We are in such a hurry that at times we even destroy the gifts. With patience and endurance, open your gifts and save the wrapping papers as well.

European Ashram, Bad Antogast, Germany
December 24, 1997

*I*n surrender the head bends and meets the heart. The head that does not bend has no value, and the head that is stiff will have to bend sooner or later, either in surrender or in shame. The head that bends in surrender will never have to bend in shame. Shame accompanies arrogance. Shyness accompanies love. See how children are endowed with shyness? That is natural. Shyness is inherent. Shame is inflicted by society and is acquired. Shame brings guilt but shyness adds to your beauty. Retain your shyness and drop your shame.

London, United Kingdom
August 22, 1996

*K*rishna tells Arjuna, "You are very dear to me" and then he tells Arjuna that he must surrender. Surrender begins with an assumption. You must assume that you are the most beloved of the Divine and then surrender happens.

Surrender is not an action; it is an assumption. Non-surrender is ignorance. Non-surrender is an illusion. Surrender begins as an assumption; then it reveals itself as a reality; and finally, it reveals itself as an illusion because there is no two, no duality. There is no independent existence for anyone, so there is nothing to surrender and nothing to surrender to. You must go through surrender absolutely to realize it is an illusion. The choice is your destiny. Krishna does not tell Arjuna in the beginning that he must surrender. First he says, "You are so dear to me." And then he tells him, "There is no other choice for you, you must surrender. Either you do it now, or you do it later." This is the path of love.

Lake Tahoe, California, United States
July 9, 1998

*M*ost of us come into this world with the seed in us – "It's not OK." All our lives we try to correct events, people and situations but how much can you correct? It is like trying to rearrange the clouds in the sky. This seed does not allow you to be happy, to smile from your heart, to be loving and loveable. It is there all the time like a thorn – irritating, irritating. This seed – "It's not OK" – brings you back into this world again and again.

So how do you burn this seed? Simply recognize that it is there. This can happen in deep introspection and meditation.

Sometimes you also feel that your body, mind, intellect, memory and ego are not OK. You justify them or find fault with them, but these are also part of the world. Acknowledge what you see as an imperfection and offer it to the Divine.

Have faith in the infinite organizing power of the Supreme Intelligence and have the sincere feeling, "Let Thy will be done." Then the seed – "It's not OK" – gets burned. "Thy will be done" is a state of total contentment, a state of complete love. We need not even make it a statement about the future: "Thy will alone is happening now."

Question: "So everything that is happening is God's will?"

Yes, including the thought – "This shouldn't be happening."

Montreal Ashram, Quebec, Canada
October 21, 1998

*T*he main impediment for many seekers on the path is that they want to surrender. Do not say that you want to surrender. Just know that you already are surrendered.

Wanting to surrender becomes an obstacle on the path. This is like a child saying to his mother, "I want to love you." No child ever says this; the child's love is self-evident.

Surrender is not an act; it is a state of your being. Whether you acknowledge it or not, surrender is there. The wise wake up and see this; the less wise take a longer time.

Know that you have no choice; you are in a state of surrender deep within you.

Chandigarh, India
March 23, 2000

Setting a time-bound goal gives direction to your life force, but imagination is essential for this. Most people have little imagination, get stuck, and end up frustrated. But if you are a devotee, you say "Let Thy will be done" and then you step lightly toward the goal. You will accomplish it with ease.

But we must make a distinction: some people say, "Let God do everything and surrender" while others say, "I must be totally responsible." Surrender is saying, "Let Thy will be done" and "Thy will" means that you take responsibility for the whole world. This appears to be contradictory and in conflict. Yet in fact, they are two sides of the same coin. The more you surrender, the more responsible you become.

One who is irresponsible cannot surrender. Why is someone irresponsible? They are lazy or fearful or both. If you are lazy or fearful, you cannot be in love.

Total responsibility is total surrender. It is a little hard to chew but this is the truth. People usually say either "I take responsibility" or "I surrender," but I tell you they go hand in hand. If you are surrendered to the knowledge, you are committed to sharing it with others. You take responsibility to see that it flourishes.

When you take responsibility and you become confused or run into obstacles, remember to surrender. That simple act releases you from the weight of feeling as though you are the doer and gives you the strength to move ahead. Responsibility is the dynamic expression of life in the present moment. When you are shaken, remember the foundation of responsibility is surrender.

Taking full responsibility and surrendering without doership are the skills of the wise. Total irresponsibility is impossible for you. Limited responsibility makes you weak. A little water in the sun will evaporate but the ocean never dries up. Limited responsibility tires you. Unlimited responsibility empowers you and brings you joy.

San Jose, California, United States
July 11, 1996

Self-reliance requires enormous courage but surrender takes less courage. A person who cannot surrender cannot be self-reliant. Just as fifty dollars contains ten dollars, so self-reliance contains surrender. If you do not have a hundred dollars, you cannot have a thousand dollars. If you do not have enough courage to surrender, then it is impossible for you to be self-reliant. People who are afraid to surrender are simply fooling themselves, because even a little fear is detrimental to self-reliance.

Often people think that surrender is a way to escape from responsibility so they end up blaming the Divine for all their problems. In fact, true surrender is taking total responsibility for everything. How? Take full responsibility and then pray for help. Surrender eventually leads you to self-reliance because there is nothing other than the Self.

Lake Lucerne, Switzerland
December 25, 1996

*I*n the word, bhakti, there are four letters: "bha" "ka" "ta" and "i" (ee). "Bha" means fulfillment and nourishment. "Ka" means knowing, or a method of knowing. "Ta" means tarana, or redeeming, saving, salvation. "I" (ee) means shakti, or energy.

So there are four components to bhakti: fulfillment and nourishment, a means of knowing, salvation, and energy. Bhakti saves you. Bhakti nourishes you. Bhakti is a way of knowing the right knowledge. When bhakti is present, doubts do not arise. Bhakti gives the most energy. Bhakti contains the seed of all four of these qualities.

All the emotional upheavals you undergo are because you do not know bhakti. When all your intense feelings flow in one direction that is bhakti.

What is the difference between a river and a flooded field? When the water flows outside its banks, it is a flood. But when the water flows within its banks, it is a river. When your emotions get flooded everywhere, the mind is in a mess. But when the emotions flow intensely in one direction, that is bhakti and that is most powerful.

A sign of intelligence is surrender or bhakti.

Trinidad, Caribbean
January 15, 1997

*A*ll the problems that you face in life are because you attach too much importance to events. The events grow large while you remain small.

Imagine you are riding a motorcycle on a busy road and in front of you there is a vehicle emitting noxious exhaust fumes. There are three options. You can remain behind the vehicle, complain and somehow bear it. You can slow down or wait, allowing the vehicle to move far ahead. Or you can use your skill, overtake the vehicle and forget about it.

As in the first option, most of you get obsessed with the events and remain miserable, inhaling fumes throughout your journey. In the second option, you usually will not get permanent relief, as another bigger vehicle is likely to move in front of you. Shying away from events is not a permanent solution.

Wise people use their skill and grow beyond the events. If your vehicle is in perfect condition, skill is effective. Conditioning the vehicle is sadhana, or spiritual practices, and skill is the grace of the master.

Bangalore Ashram, India
December 14, 1995

*I*f you pour water into a poorly fired clay pot, the pot breaks and the water is wasted. If the pot is well fired and strong, then it does not matter whether you put water into the pot or put the pot into water.

Bangalore Ashram, India
September 12, 1996

*F*ocus sharpens the mind and relaxation expands the mind. An expanded mind without sharpness cannot bring holistic development. At the same time, a sharp mind without expansion causes tension, anger and frustration.

The balance of a focused mind and an expanded consciousness brings perfection. Sudarshan Kriya and the advanced course techniques aim at developing consciousness that is sharp and unbounded. Seva and commitment play a major role in this, as do the food you eat and your attitude in daily life.

Expanded consciousness is peace and joy. Focused consciousness is love and creativity. A point of focused consciousness is individual self. When every atom of the expanded consciousness becomes sharp and focused, that is the awakening of Divinity.

Bangalore Ashram, India
November 26, 1998

126

*Y*agnas are the ancient method of enriching the subtle; they purify the individual as well as the collective consciousness.

Yagna has three aspects:

- Deva puja – Acknowledging and honoring the Divine in all its forms.

- Sangatikarana – Hastening the process of evolution by bringing together all the elements and people in creation.

- Dana – Sharing and giving what you have been blessed with.

Bangalore Ashram, India
October 8, 1997

*Y*agna creates energy and energy creates consciousness, awareness. Heightened awareness brings you close to reality and reality is a witness.

To realize that everything is happening you need heightened awareness. And to bring about heightened awareness you have to increase prana.

Prana can be increased through:

- Fasting and fresh food
- Cold water baths
- Total exhaustion, not letting sleep take over
- Emotional peaks
- Singing and chanting
- Pranayamas, Kriya and meditation
- Giving without givership, serving without doership
- The presence of the master
- Silence

All of these together are yagna.

Lonay, Lake Geneva, Switzerland
October 7, 1998

*T*o the degree that you are awake, everything around you brings knowledge. If you are not awake, even the most precious knowledge does not make sense.

Awareness depends upon your ability to open and shut your windows. When there is a storm, you need to shut your windows – otherwise you will get wet. When it is hot and suffocating inside, you need to open your windows.

Your senses are like windows. When you are awake and you have the ability to open and shut your windows at will, then you are free. If your windows cannot be shut or opened at will, you are bound. Attending to this is sadhana.

Stockholm, Sweden
August 13, 1997

*D*ifferent organs of your body are governed by different devas. The solar plexus is connected with the sun – which is why it is called "solar" plexus. The solar plexus has a profound impact on the central nervous system, the optic nerves, the stomach and what we usually call our "gut feeling." It is the second brain in your body.

Usually the solar plexus is slightly bigger than an almond. But with the practice of yoga, meditation and Sudarshan Kriya, the solar plexus can become as large as a human hand. It can then balance the bodily functions. When the solar plexus expands, the intuitive mind improves and the mind becomes clear and focused. When the solar plexus contracts, you feel miserable, sad, depressed, and all sorts of negative feelings come.

When the first rays of the sun fall on the solar plexus, it is beneficial for your body. Doing Surya Namaskar yoga asana – sun salutation – in the early morning is an excellent way to expand the solar plexus.

Krishna was called Padmanabha, which means "whose navel is the size of a lotus flower." If you become Padmanabha, you become absolutely creative. Brahma, the Creator, is born out of a blossomed solar plexus.

European Ashram, Bad Antogast, Germany
January 8, 1997

*I*f you are unable to meditate because your mind is chattering, just feel that you are a little stupid, and then you will be able to sink deep into meditation. Your intellect is a small portion of your total consciousness. If you are stuck in the intellect, you miss a great deal. Happiness is when you transcend the intellect. In awe or in feeling stupid, you transcend the intellect.

Baltimore, Maryland, United States
June 17, 1998

*W*hat is boredom? Boredom is a repetition without interest or love that causes a monotonous state of mind. Boredom overshadows the Self.

A practice or abhyasa is repetition whose purpose is to destroy the boredom and reunite with the Self. In this process the practice itself creates boredom and as you continue, it penetrates the boredom and destroys it once and for all. Whether the practice gives you joy or boredom, it must be continued. Only the practice or abhyasa can annihilate the mind. The Self is love and love is always repetitive. That is why love letters are repetitive but there is no boredom for the lovers.

If you are bored with yourself just imagine how much more boring you are for others. Root out boredom through deep and continued meditation.

Bangalore Ashram, India
November 15, 1995

*O*nly a conscious, alert and dynamic person can get bored; a dull and inert person does not. If you get bored, it indicates you are more alive and human. It is a sign that you are growing, that you are evolving.

An animal, for example, keeps doing the same thing. It never gets bored. Cows, horses, birds do the same things over and over throughout their lives.

People eat, watch television, change jobs, change partners to escape boredom. Then they become frustrated and this frustration takes them back to inertia and unconsciousness.

Only in two states does boredom not occur: in a state of total inertia or in a state of Divine consciousness. If you are bored, it indicates you are evolving. Boredom moves you. Be proud of your boredom and celebrate!

Arenal Volcano, Tabacon, Costa Rica
June 16, 1999

*D*issolving the name is awareness.
Dissolving the form is meditation.
The world is name and form.
Bliss transcends name and form.

Bangalore Ashram, India
September 24, 1997

*Y*ou can only seek that which you know and when you really understand, you already have it, so it need not be sought. You cannot seek something you do not know.

Whatever you seek and whenever you seek it, it is always only One and the One is what you are already.

So, you cannot seek something you do not know and when you know what you are seeking, you already have it. When you seek the world, you get misery and when you want to find your way out of misery, you find the Divine.

A man lost a penny and was looking for it in a bush when he found a huge treasure. He was not seeking for treasure but only for his lost penny. In the same way, when you seek one thing you may get something else and it may be much greater than what you lost.

The truth, or Self, cannot be sought directly.

Taipei, Taiwan
May 17, 2000

*T*here are six signs of a seeker.

First, acknowledge that you know very little. Many people think they know without really knowing or they become trapped in their limited knowledge so they never learn. Thus the first thing is to acknowledge that you know very little.

Second, be willing to know. Many people acknowledge that they know very little, but they still may not be ready to learn.

Third, be nonjudgmental and open-minded. Some would like to learn, but their judgmental attitude and close-mindedness do not allow them to learn.

Fourth, be totally committed to the path. Some are open-minded but they lack commitment and one-pointedness. They keep shopping here and there and never progress.

Fifth, always place truth and service before pleasure. Sometimes even committed and one-pointed people avoid the path in pursuit of momentary pleasures.

Finally, have patience and perseverance. Some people are committed and one-pointed and are not swayed by pleasures, but if they lack patience and perseverance, they become restless and dejected.

Bangalore Ashram, India
October 1, 1997

*T*he mind that seeks pleasure cannot be centered. You either seek pleasure or you come to me. When you are centered, all pleasures come to you anyway, but they are no longer pleasures. They lose their charm. If you enjoy your suffering, then again, you cannot be centered and you are far from the path. The mind that seeks pleasure or enjoys suffering can never achieve the highest. If you are after pleasure, forget about satsang. Why are you wasting your time? This is the Art of Living.

Bangalore Ashram, India
December 12, 1996

*W*hat time do you give the Divine? Usually you give the time that is left over, when you have nothing else to do, when no guests are coming, there are no parties to attend, no nice movies to watch, no weddings in which to participate. Such time you give freely but this is not quality time.

Give quality time to the Divine; it will be rewarded. If your prayers are not answered, it is because you have never given quality time. Give Satsang and meditation your highest priority.

Kauai, Hawaii, United States
January 24, 1996

*W*hy do people need homes? Can they live like animals in the forest without shelter? Humans need protection from changing nature, so they build shelters for physical comfort. In the same way, for spiritual and mental comfort, satsang is the shelter.

One who does not do satsang is like a wild animal. Satsang alone makes you civilized. Satsang is the shelter from changing time and its harsh influence on life. Satsang is the nest in which you can find repose. If you are a taker of happiness, you receive misery. If you are a giver of happiness, you receive joy and love.

Calcutta, India
April 17, 1997

*T*here is an ancient Sanskrit proverb that says the words of rishis and enlightened ones are immediately translated into experience.

Your whole body is made up of atoms. Being with this truth kindles energy in you and elevates your consciousness. When you sing bhajans, the sound energy gets absorbed into every atom of your body. Just as a microphone absorbs sound and converts it into electricity, the body absorbs sound and converts it into consciousness. When you sit in bhajans, your entire body gets soaked in energy and transformation happens. If you are sitting and listening to gossip or violent music, then that gets absorbed by your body. But when you hear the knowledge, or chant with all your heart, your consciousness is elevated.

Bangalore Ashram, India
May 14, 1999

*W*e usually do only that which is purposeful, useful and rational. Everything you see is seen through the rational mind. But intuition, discovery, new knowledge go beyond the rational mind. Truth is beyond the rational mind. The rational mind is like a railroad track that is fixed in grooves. An airplane has no tracks; it can fly anywhere. A balloon can float anywhere.

Some people step out of the rational mind in order to rebel against society. They want to break social law for the sake of their egos. They do it out of anger, hatred, rebelliousness and to attract attention. This is not stepping out of the rational mind, though they may think it is.

We step out of the rational mind when we do something that has no purpose. Accepting that, as an act, makes it a game. Life becomes lighter. If you are stuck with only rational acts, life becomes a burden. Suppose you play a game without a thought to winning or losing, just acting irrationally. Performing an act without any purpose attached to it is freedom, like a dance. So just step out of the rational mind. You will find greater freedom, an unfathomable depth, and you will come face to face with reality. Reality transcends logic and the rational mind. Until you transcend the rational mind, you will not gain access to creativity and the infinite.

But if you perform an irrational act in order to find freedom, then it already has a purpose and a meaning. It is no longer irrational. It has already spoiled its own possibility.

Break through the barrier of the rational mind and find freedom for yourself.

New York City, New York, United States
June 10, 1998

137

*E*ducation has five aspects:

♦ Information – Often we think that information is education, but it is only one aspect of education.

♦ Concepts – Concepts are the basis for all research. You need to conceive of something in order to create.

♦ Attitude – An integral aspect of education is cultivating the right attitude. Proper attitude at the right time and the right place determines your actions and behavior.

♦ Imagination – Imagination is essential for creativity, for the arts. But if you get stuck in imagination, you can become psychotic.

♦ Freedom – Freedom is your very nature. Only with freedom do joy, generosity and other human values blossom. Without freedom, imagination becomes stagnant, attitudes become stifling, concepts become a burden and information is of no value.

Bangalore Ashram, India
June 7, 2000

*O*ne who has given everything has also given freedom. Honor the freedom first and make good use of all things given to you.

Bangalore Ashram, India
October 16, 1996

*T*o think fresh you need to be free of all impressions. Let go of all impressions right this moment and be hollow and empty. When you hear a word, the sound instantaneously conveys the meaning. Similarly, the knowledge that you are sitting, standing or talking needs neither confirmation nor proof.

Just an intention to be free makes you immediately free.

Realizing that freedom is your very nature brings enormous shakti – energy.

Pandalam, Kerala, India
December 2, 1999

*T*he full moon of Raksha Bandhan is dedicated to the seers – the rishis. Bandhan means bondage; raksha means protection. This is a bondage that protects you. Your bondage to the knowledge, to the master, to truth, to the Self, all save you. A rope can be tied to either protect or strangle you. The small mind and mundane things can strangle you. The Big Mind and knowledge save you. Raksha Bandhan is the bondage that saves you.

You are bound by your bondage to satsang. Your bondage to the master, to truth, to the ancient knowledge of the rishis is your savior. Bonding is essential in life. Let the bonding be divine in a life free from bondage.

Denmark
August 20, 1997

*F*reedom and discipline are opposites and complementary. The purpose of defense is to protect freedom. But is there freedom in defense? Do soldiers have freedom? No, they are totally bound, not even allowed to move the right foot when told to put the left foot down. Their steps are measured and they are unable to even walk with a natural rhythm. There is total lack of freedom in defense. That which has absolutely no freedom is protecting the freedom of the country! So it is with the police; they protect the freedom of the individual. But are they free?

Discipline protects freedom. They go hand in hand. Understand this and go forward in life. You have some restrictions and this is what allows you freedom. You can choose to focus either on freedom or discipline, and this makes you happy or unhappy. Freedom without discipline is like a country without defense.

Fences should be fences; a fence cannot be built everywhere on your property. If your fence is everywhere, how can you build a house? The state of high absolute freedom is too difficult; we need to be very practical. Yes, there is a state of unlimited bliss, the freedom Advaita talks about. But Advaita knowledge has been totally misused or used to promote one's own whims and conveniences.

There must be awareness in the mind, love in the heart, and righteousness in action. Love and fear are two possibilities that put you on track. Some religions use fear to improve life. At a certain age, nature induces fear in a child. Before that, a child gets all of the mother's time and love – the child has no fear. As the child grows more independent, it becomes cautious. Nature brings in an iota of fear. With freedom, the child starts walking carefully. Fear of losing freedom also brings defense; the purpose of defense is to eliminate fear.

On this path, knowledge is your freedom and also your defense.

Bangalore Ashram, India
October 10, 1995

*P*eople who are free regret that they do not have discipline. They keep promising that they will become disciplined. People who are disciplined look for the end of it because discipline is not an end in itself, it is a means.

Look at people who have no discipline; they are miserable. Freedom without discipline is absolute misery. Discipline without freedom is suffocating. Orderliness is monotonous and chaos is stressful. We must make discipline free and freedom disciplined.

Those who are with other people all the time, look for the comforts of solitude. Those who are in solitude feel lonely and want to be with others. Those who are in a cold place want to be in a warm place. Those who are in a warm place love something cool. This is the dilemma of life: everyone is looking for perfect balance. Perfect balance is like a razor's edge. It can only be found in the Self.

European Ashram, Bad Antogast, Germany
October 2, 1996

*I*nitiation is called diksha. In Sanskrit "di" means intellect. "Ksha" means the horizon or the end. Diksha means going to the end of intellect – transcending the intellect.

Education is called shiksha, the horizon of discipline – total discipline. Discipline is needed for education. Diksha is needed for meditation.

A teacher provides shiksha. A guru provides diksha. A guru takes you beyond the intellect to the realm of being. It is a journey from the head to the heart.

Blossoming beyond the intellect is diksha. If you do not go beyond the intellect, you will not smile, you will not laugh. Once diksha happens, you are happy, blissful and contented; and your thirst for knowledge is quenched.

Totality of discipline is shiksha. Totality of intelligence is diksha.

Calcutta, India
February 25, 1999

*L*ike fish in water,
You are in air and
Thoughts are in the mind.
Mind is in the Big Mind.
The Big Mind in me is love.
Emotions are ripples in love.
Love is all knowledge.

Every atom of the Big Mind is crammed with knowledge.
Knowing this, you stop seeking. You seek until you come to the
master. You walk until you come to the swimming pool but you
do not walk or run in the pool – you swim or float. Once you
come to the master, seeking stops and blossoming begins.

You are knowledge. Every atom in you is shimmering with
knowledge. This is called "go." "Go" has four meanings:
knowledge, movement, achievement, and freedom or liberation.
"Pal" means friend or protector – one who takes care. Be a
gopal. Be a friend in knowledge.

Often you become friends by gossiping about negative things,
complaining together, having similar cravings or aversions,
sharing common enemies or common problems, or sharing
common goals or common addictions.

Coming together in knowledge is rare. You become friends
because you have something in common. Be a friend in
knowledge. Uplift each other in knowledge. Those who attend
satsang are gopals – reminding each other, coming together in
and for knowledge. That is gopal, a protector of this
knowledge.

Melbourne, Australia
September 13, 1995

143

*K*nowledge is a burden
    if it robs you of innocence.
Knowledge is a burden
    if it makes you feel you are special.
Knowledge is a burden
    if it gives you an idea that you are wise.
Knowledge is a burden
    if it is not integrated into life.
Knowledge is a burden
    if it does not bring you joy.
Knowledge is a burden
    if it does not set you free.

Bangalore Ashram, India
August 19, 1999

*I*f you are in love with the Divine, then you can digest
knowledge. Love is the appetizer – seva is the exercise.
Without love and seva, knowledge becomes indigestible.

Los Angeles, California, United States
January 30, 1997

*E*verything here is recycled. The earth is millions of years old – the Alps, the water, the air. Billions of people have breathed the same air.

You are recycled. All the particles in your body are old, your thoughts and emotions are recycled, your mind is recycled.

Consciousness is recycled – it is the same old consciousness.

Remind yourself that everything here is recycled material – so relax! Everything goes from whence it came. Recycling brings back purity and hygiene.

Knowledge recycles the mind. Knowledge keeps everything fresh. That is why you can keep recycling the same creation. A mind in knowledge finds everything fresh. If you do not put knowledge into your mind, the mind gets rotten. Knowledge brings the mind back to purity. Recycling brings purity.

European Ashram, Bad Antogast, Germany
December 30, 1998

Question: "Guruji, what is your message?"

I have no message. In order to give a message you have to be far away. A message needs distance. A message is of the past or of the future. A message is impersonal and lifeless. Knowledge cannot be a message. The wise one will not give you a message but will simply awaken you.

God will not give you a message. For God to give you a message, God has to be far away from you. God is closer to you than your breath. How can He give you a message?

The wise neither need a message nor give a message. Whoever needs the message will not use it. And one who can use the message will not need it.

Question: "What is the difference between knowledge and a message?"

You can read the ingredients – read a message – but when you taste the food, the information becomes knowledge. You can read about living in the moment again and again, but it only becomes knowledge when you experience it.

Salvador Bahia, Brazil
June 9, 1999

*K*nowledge has an end. Knowledge completes. So also does discipleship, for the goal of the disciple is to acquire knowledge.

Once you cross the water, however nice the boat is, you get off the boat. After twelve years, the disciple completes his studies. The master does a ceremony called Samavartha, where he tells the disciple that he is ending the discipleship and asks him to behave at par with him and let the Brahman dynamically manifest.

Sakha is a companion in life and death; it never ends. In the path of love there is neither beginning nor end. Sakha only wants the beloved. Sakha does not care about knowledge or liberation. Love is incomplete because of longing and so it is infinite, for infinity can never be complete.

Arjuna was a sakha to Krishna and although Krishna was the perfect master he was also a sakha. What are you, a shishya – a disciple, or a sakha – a companion?

Halifax, Nova Scotia, Canada
October 17, 1995

*T*here are three things: the Self, the senses, and the object or the world. And there are three words: sukha, pleasure; dukha, sorrow; and sakha, companion. These have one thing in common: "kha" which means senses.

The Self experiences the world through the senses. When the senses are with the Self, that is pleasure, or sukha, because the Self is the source of all joy or pleasure. When the senses are distant from the Self, or dukha – in the mud, lost in the object – that is misery. Mud, misery, mind – they are very close.

Self is the nature of joy. You close your eyes during any pleasant experience – as you smell a nice flower, or as you taste or touch something. Sukha is that which takes you to the Self. Dukha is that which takes you away from the Self. Sorrow simply means that you are caught up in the object which changes, instead of focusing on the Self which is non-changing. All the sense objects are just a diving board to take you back to the Self.

Sakha – companion – means "He is the senses." Sakha is one who has become your senses, who is your senses. If you are my senses, it means I get knowledge through you; you are my sixth sense. As I trust my mind, so I trust you. A friend could be just an object of the senses, but a sakha has become your very own senses.

Sakha is the companion who is there in both the experiences of dukha – self – and of sukha – pleasure. Sakha is one who leads you back to the Self. If you are stuck in an object, the wisdom that pulls you back to the Self is sakha.

Knowledge is your companion and the master is nothing but the embodiment of knowledge. So sakha means, "He is my senses, I see the world through that wisdom, through him."

If your senses are with the Divine, then you see the whole world through the Divinity. Your head will be in the mud in a few years; do not put mud in your head while you are still alive.

Montreal Ashram, Quebec, Canada
October 24, 1995

*D*o not follow me. In fact, you cannot follow me, because I am behind you. I am behind you to push you forward. You have to leave everything behind and move ahead. Everything – all your experiences, your relations – everything is part of the past. Drop everything. Leave the whole world of your memories behind, including me.

Move on and be free. Stop looking for more; then you will be free and compassion will flow from you.

There is one kind of "do not follow me" that comes from fear or rebelliousness. The other kind of "do not follow me" comes from a heightened awareness.

You cannot follow me because I am behind you and I am in you. For too long you have been following as a sheep; now it is time to be a lion.

Zen Monastery, Blois, France
April 22, 1998

*T*he master is a doorway. To bring you to the doorway, it must be more charming than the world. Imagine someone in the street – there is rain, thunder; they need shelter. They look around, they find a doorway and they come to it. The doorway is more inviting, more charming, more celebrative, more joyful than anything else in the world.

Nothing in the world can give that much peace, joy and pleasure. Once you come to the doorway, you enter the door and see the world from there; you see the world from the eyes of the master. This is a sign that you have come to the master. Otherwise you will remain standing in the street, looking at the door.

But once you have entered the door you will see the whole world from the eyes of the master. And what does this mean? In every situation that you face, you will think, "If the master faced this situation, how would he handle it?" "If someone blames the master like this, what would he do?"

See the world from the eyes of the master at all times. The world looks so much more beautiful – not a nasty place, but a place filled with love, joy, cooperation, compassion and all virtues. The world is so much more fun. Looking back through the doorway, there is no fear. You will have relationships with everybody without any fear because you have shelter.

From inside your home, you will look at the thunder; you will look at the storm, at the rain, at the bright sun. Inside you have air conditioning – it is very cool and pleasant. Outside it is hot and uncomfortable but you do not mind because there is nothing that can distract you, disturb you, or take the fullness away from you. Such a sense of security, such a sense of fullness and joy come. That is the purpose of having a master.

All relationships in the world go awry. You make relationships and you break them. All relationships can get broken, fixed, and broken again. There is craving and aversion. This is the world; this is samsara. But the master is not a relationship. The master is a presence.

What must you do to feel the presence of the master, to avoid making it a relationship? Do not make the master a part of your world. If you make him a part of the world, the same emotional garbage arises. "Oh, he said this." "He did not say that." "Somebody is close." "I am not close." Just feel the presence of the master; that is eternal. That has been there with you before, is there now, and will be there in the future.

The master is the presence. The world is relativity and relativity has limitations. Presence is unlimited. Presence is vast, infinite and comprehensive – all-inclusive. And the presence of the master in one's life will bring fulfillment to all relations. Every relationship will become complete with the presence of Infinity if the master is in your life.

Montreal Ashram, Quebec, Canada
July 12, 1995

*I*f you are not feeling close to the master, it is because of you, because of your mind, because of your ego concepts. Share with the guru that which is very important or intimate to you. Do not feel shame, shy, or judgmental about yourself. Unless you express to the master that which is very intimate and important to you, just being on the formal and informal communication levels cannot make you feel close. "How are you? Where are you going? How have you been?" Stop formal and superficial conversations with the master and speak with your heart that which is very important and intimate, very deep to your life. Do not just say unimportant, mundane things.

If you do not feel close to the master, there is no point in having a master. It is just another burden to you. You have enough already. Just say, "Goodbye," be rid of it.

You are with the master to share the joy of the master, to share the consciousness of the master. For that, you have to empty your cup of what is already in it and you share that with the master. You share whatever you have and do not judge, "Oh, that is garbage." The master is ready to accept any garbage of any extent. However you are, he will embrace you. He is ready to share. You only have to share from your side.

Big Sur, California, United States
June 21, 1995

*I*n the presence of your satguru, knowledge flourishes; sorrow diminishes; without any reason, joy wells up; lack diminishes; abundance dawns; and all talents manifest.

To the degree you feel connected to your guru, these qualities manifest in your life.

Bangalore Ashram, India
September 24, 1997

*O*ften what is universal is not personal and what is personal does not belong to everyone. What is "mine" and what is "universal" are completely opposite. This is the cause of greed, fear, jealousy and lack of contentment. On this Guru Purnima wake up and realize that the Lord of the Universe is very personal to you. Your personal guru is the guru of the whole world. The guru is your very Self and your Self is the very life in every being. Make the universal personal; it makes you richer, wiser, stronger. Make the personal universal; you will find freedom, compassion and love.

Tahoe City, California, United States
July 23, 1997

*O*nce a master was traveling in the middle province of India with a disciple following him a few yards behind. Some boys who were rude, rough and abusive began to throw stones and tease the disciple, calling him names. This went on for some time as the boys followed the master and the disciple. They came to a river. The master and the disciple got into a boat in order to cross. The boys got into another boat and as they reached the middle of the river the boat began to sink.

The master slapped the disciple across the face. The disciple was so surprised as he had not said a word to the boys in response to their taunts. He had been such a good disciple and yet the master had slapped him!

The master said, "It is your fault. You are responsible for their boat sinking. You did not respond to their abuse. Nature has now punished them in a worse way because you did not have enough compassion to quell their insults."

With that slap the master took away the karma of this event so that it would not be carried into the boys' future. It also served to take away any little bit of joy the disciple may have felt at seeing the boys' boat sink. Thus, it also took away the karma of the event for the disciple. So the anger of the enlightened is a blessing.

Here and now
August 31, 1995

A builder of temples uses all types of stones. He uses certain stones for the foundation; these never appear outside. From other stones, he makes the walls and pillars of the temple. From yet other stones he makes the steps and other stones become the tower of the temple. Only the finest stones that are suitable for carving will become the Deity and will be installed in the temple. When the stone becomes a part of the temple, it no longer remains a stone; it becomes a sculpture, a piece of art, it becomes the living Deity.

In the same way many people come to the master. According to the degree of their surrender they are installed by the master. All are essential. If there were no steps, how could a person reach the temple? If there were no foundation, how could the temple be there at all? What can a tower do without pillars? For a builder of temples, each stone is precious and valuable.

Montreal, Canada
June 10, 1997

155

*B*reak through all your barriers and feel that you are blessed. This is the one and only step you have to take – the rest will all happen spontaneously.

This deep sense of feeling that "I am blessed" can help you overcome any obstacles in life. It gives you courage and confidence and it will open you up for grace to pour in.

Once you realize that you are blessed, then all complaints disappear, all grumbling vanishes, all insecurities evaporate, the sense of feeling unloved dissolves, and the desire for love fades.

If you do not realize you are blessed, then doership begins. If you want to make a difference in your life, feel you are blessed. Especially for those on this path of knowledge, there is no reason for you to not feel blessed.

So, feel you are blessed and take the first step towards the Self.

National Highway 7, Between Bangalore and Shimoga, India
October 23, 1997

CHAPTER THREE

You, God and Beyond

*C*elebration is the nature of the spirit.
   Any celebration must be spiritual.
A celebration without spirituality has no depth.
Silence gives depth to celebration.

Some people think being silent is spirituality. Many meditators feel that laughing, singing and dancing are not spiritual. Some people think only celebration is spirituality. In some parts of the world – rural India or Africa – celebration means loud music; there is no silence at all. But spirituality is a harmonious blend of outer silence and inner celebration, as well as inner silence and outer celebration.

Bangalore Ashram, India
October 20, 1999

*T*here are three forces in nature: Brahma shakti, Vishnu shakti and Shiva shakti. Usually one of these predominates in you. Brahma shakti is the force that creates something new; Vishnu shakti is the force of maintenance; and Shiva shakti is the force that brings transformation, infusion of life, or destruction.

Some of you have Brahma shakti. You may create well, but you cannot maintain what you create. You may make friends very quickly, but the friendships do not last long.

Others among you have Vishnu shakti. You cannot create but you are good at maintenance. You have long-lasting friendships but you cannot make any new friends.

And then there are others who have more Shiva shakti. These people bring new life or cause transformation, or they destroy what has been done.

In guru shakti, all three shaktis have fully blossomed.

First, identify which shakti predominates in you and then aspire for guru shakti.

Bangalore Ashram, India
November 23, 1995

*T*he whole world functions according to laws of Nature, moving in an auspicious rhythm of innocence and intelligence. That auspiciousness is Divinity. Shiva is harmonious innocence that knows no control.

Control is Vashi, the reverse of Shiva. Control is of the mind. Control means two, duality, weakness. Vashi is not doing something naturally, but exerting pressure. Often people think they are in control of their lives, their situation, but control is an illusion. Control is a temporary exertion of energy in the mind. That is Vashi.

Shiva is the opposite. Shiva is the permanent and eternal source of energy, the eternal state of Being, the One without a second.

Duality is the cause of fear and that harmonious innocence dissolves duality.

When the moment is whole, complete, then that moment is Divine. Being in the moment means no regret for the past, no want for the future. Time stops, mind stops.

Bangalore Ashram, India
February 24, 1998

*E*very cell in your body has the ability of all five senses. You can see without the eyes; vision is part of consciousness, which is why in dreams you can see without the eyes. There is an expression "looking with a thousand eyes" – you are all eyes.

You can feel without the skin. That is why someone who has lost a leg can still feel sensations in his missing limb. You can smell without the nose and taste without the tongue. When someone says something, you are all ears – you are listening with every cell of your body.

The five senses and the ability to think are all present in consciousness. So each cell of the body has the potential to perform all the functions of the senses. All cells are made of the same tissue – each DNA molecule contains all functions of the body. Consciousness is inherent in all cells and every sensory stimulus brings knowledge, which is the nature of consciousness.

New Millennium Course, Carrara, Italy
December 30, 1999

A single cell becomes the whole body. Somewhere it becomes fingernails, somewhere it becomes the nose and tongue, but everything is a manifestation of a single cell. In the same way, the entire universe is made up of a single substance.

Remembering and feeling that everything is made up of one thing heals the body and mind and balances the three doshas in the body – vata, pitta and kapha. This is savitarka samadhi, which means equanimity with logical awareness.

Deep sleep can be jada samadhi – equanimity with inertia. Hence sleep is the main factor in healing. Even medicines will not help without sleep and rest.

Samadhi with ecstasy has no logic. This is nirvitarka samadhi, awareness with bliss. Nirvitarka samadhi is beyond the experience of bliss, indefinable beyond words.

den Haag, Netherlands
May 29, 1996

*B*liss cannot be understood and it is extremely difficult to achieve. After many lifetimes you finally achieve bliss, but once achieved, it is even more difficult to lose. All that you seek in your life is bliss, that divine union with your source, and everything else in the world distracts you from that goal. There are a million things to distract you from that goal in so many ways – so many unexplainable, incomprehensible ways of not coming home.

The mind is kept alive by cravings and aversions. Only when the mind dies does bliss dawn. Bliss is the abode of all divinity, all devas. It is only possible to comprehend bliss, to uphold it in this human body. And having had a human life and having known this path, if you still do not realize this, you are at the greatest loss.

Cravings and aversions make your heart hard. There is no use being polite in your behavior if you are rough in your heart. If your behavior is rude it is acceptable, but not if you are rough in your heart. The world does not care how you are inside. It will only see your behavior. But the Divine does not care how you are outside – He only looks within. Never let even a small amount of dislike or craving reside in your heart. Let it be fresh, soft and fragrant like a rose.

It is such an illusion – you dislike someone or something, and this only makes you hard and your hardness takes a long time to soften, to disappear. Cravings and aversions are traps that prevent you from finding the treasure.

Nothing in this material world can give you contentment. An outer-looking mind seeking for contentment gets more discontented and the discontentment grows, and complaints and negativity harden the brain, cloud the awareness, and form a cloud of negative energy. When the negativity reaches its peak, like an over-inflated balloon, it bursts and comes back to the Divinity.

You can never escape the Divine, the long route of negativity, or the instantaneous positive approach. When Divinity dawns, the shift happens from untruth to truth, from darkness to light, from dull inert matter to sparkling spirit.

European Ashram, Bad Antogast, Germany
January 6, 1999

*S*tretching sound is music.
Stretching movement is dance.
Stretching the smile is laughter.
Stretching the mind is meditation.
Stretching life is celebration.
Stretching the devotee is God.
Stretching feeling is ecstasy.
Stretching emptiness is bliss.

Emptiness is the doorway between the material and spiritual worlds. It is where you come to understand the nature of the spirit. If you do not know emptiness, then you cannot know the joy of being. Experiencing being causes emptiness. From emptiness begins fullness.

On one side of emptiness is misery and on the other side is joy. That is what Buddha meant when he said, "The whole world is misery and what is to be achieved is emptiness."

Bangalore Ashram, India
February 3, 1999

*I*ntention pushes you to the future but bliss is always in the present. The one who wakes up to this truth is wise. If an intention arises in a state of bliss, the intention can manifest effortlessly.

European Ashram, Bad Antogast, Germany
December 23, 1999

*F*or your prayer to be answered, your desire must be intense. The greater the intensity of your desire and the later it gets fulfilled, the greater will be your gratitude.

Intense desire leads you to devotion. For desire to become intense, some time and the desire are required. When an intense desire is fulfilled, gratitude is so overwhelming that its achievement loses its charm and significance.

People think that they are unfortunate if their desires are not fulfilled quickly. Intense desire can frustrate you or make you prayerful. In prayerfulness, there is gratitude and devotion.

Any intense experience makes you whole.

Calcutta, India
November 20, 1996

*A*ttaining the Divine depends on the intensity of your longing and not on the time you spend or your qualifications. A proverb among the villagers in India says, "It may take some time to pluck a flower, but it takes no time to meet the Divine." Your abilities or qualifications are not the criteria – it is simply the intensity of your longing.

Immediately intensify your longing for the Divine. This happens when you know that you are nothing and that you want nothing. Knowing that you are nothing and that you want nothing brings a sense of belonging, and belonging intensifies longing.

What is the difference between desire and longing? Desire is the fever of the head. Longing is the cry of the heart.

Bangalore Ashram, India
May 21, 1998

Organization is control. Devotion is chaos. Organization requires attention to details, a material awareness. Organization is being worldly. Devotion is getting lost, forgetting the world, being in ecstasy.

Organization and devotion are opposite in nature. They do not go together, yet they cannot be apart or exist without each other. No organization can arise without devotion. When there is so much devotion, you simply want to organize. Devotion brings faith, compassion and responsibility. With responsibility and caring, you want to give knowledge, wisdom and love. That is when organization happens. So organization exists through devotion.

If you are devoted, you will not simply sit. The nature of devotion is to give. If you think you are devoted and you are not caring for the world, then you are merely selfish. Real devotion means being one with the Divine, and the Divine cares for the world.

You often lose devotion in organizing. And often, in the name of devotion, you create chaos and disregard the organization. You have to be a saint to be both in organization and devotion.

Kauai, Hawaii, United States
February 3, 1998

*E*verything is made up of atoms. The whole world is nothing but an organization where the atoms have decided to arrange themselves in a specific pattern to form a particular substance. And those particular patterns bring with them specific qualities.

Death, decay and transformation happen when the atoms get bored with patterns and decide to reorganize themselves. When the atoms of an apple say, "Enough of being an apple," that is when the rotting starts. If there is never boredom of patterns, there can be no decay.

The movement from one organized state to another is also organized. This is the transient organization called chaos. This transient organization may need a catalyst, and knowledge is such a catalyst. So, there is absolutely no escape from organization.

Bangalore Ashram, India
December 17, 1998

*Y*ou cannot eliminate formality in society. It must be given its place. But devoid of cordiality, formality can be hypocritical. Cordiality alone may cause chaos and at times may even appear to be uncaring.

Formality improves communication; cordiality improves communion – oneness. Communication is only necessary where there are two. Formality maintains duality. Structures are based on formality. Love and knowledge are based on cordiality. For love and knowledge to blossom, you need an informal, cordial environment.

An organization cannot happen, orderliness cannot prevail, if formalities are abandoned. All actions are measured steps of formality. Devotion is informal and totally chaotic.

Cordiality is the core of one's existence; formality is the outer shell. When the outer shell is thin, it can reflect the inner light, like the shade of the lamp that softens the light. But if the lampshade is too opaque, you cannot see the light. Similarly, we must strike a balance between formality and cordiality.

Rishikesh, India
March 4, 1998

*T*he body is dependent on all of creation. In society, someone must sew clothes, produce electricity, drill for oil. The body cannot be independent of the world. For the body, dependence is absolute.

When the Spirit identifies with the body, then it gets pinched and it looks for independence. Mind, intellect, ego – they all look for independence.

168

In looking for independence you often get mired in the ego and become more miserable, but most people are not aware of their dependency. When they become aware of their limitations and dependency, the desire for independence arises.

Independence cannot be achieved unless you start moving within and when you move within, you discover that you are interdependent. The individual Self is interdependence. In fact, every wise person knows that everything is interdependent and that there is no such thing as independence.

On one level dependence is a harsh reality. On another level, it is an illusion because there is nothing but the Self. It is only when you do not feel oneness, belongingness that you want independence. Because the Self is non-dual, there is no question of dependence or independence. One who asks for independence is a beggar. One who knows that it is an illusion is a king.

When the sense of belongingness is not well-founded, the life of a seeker is volatile. The ego then finds some excuse to revert to smallness because it is not yet soaked in the totality of knowledge.

As the ego is not accustomed to belongingness, the mind finds every little excuse to revert back to the ego and to be aloof, independent and separate. It tries to find any small fault and blow it out of proportion.

Be aware of these tendencies and come what may, be strong in the commitment to satsang, to the path.

Muszyna, Poland
September 3, 1998

*T*o worship or idolize without a sense of belonging is always futile. Such worship only results in fear and distance. On the other hand, some are paranoid about worship. They get annoyed when they see others worshipping.

Modes of worshipping or idolizing are different in different parts of the world. Some worship the Pope; others worship pop stars; some are crazy about politicians. Look at the children; they worship their heroes on posters all over the walls. But adoration alone makes you a fan. A sense of belonging and seeing the divinity in those whom you adore makes you a saint. Those who worship without a sense of belonging and those who are against worship are in the same boat; both are clogged with fear.

The Bible says, "I am your God. You shall have no other gods before me." The same is said in the ancient Indian scriptures. "One who worships God as separate from the 'I am' consciousness is dull-headed," and "Poojo aur na deva" – do not worship other gods.

The offering, the offered and the offerer are all One.

Bangalore Ashram, India
February 10, 2000

*T*he role of religion is to make us righteous and loving, and the purpose of politics is to care for people and their welfare. When religion and politics do not coexist, then you have corrupt politicians and pseudo-religious leaders.

A religious man who is righteous and loving will definitely care for the welfare of the whole population and hence becomes a true politician. All the avatars and prophets cared for people and so were political. And a true politician can only be righteous and loving so he cannot be anything but religious.

When religions restrict freedom to worship and restrict modes of worship, they become unsuitable for creating a harmonious society. When religion becomes all encompassing and gives full freedom to pray and worship in any manner – that religion will bring righteousness and peace in people and will be suitable for any society.

People think that politics and religion have to be kept separate because many religions did not allow freedom of worship and did not care equally for all people. History has shown that religion has created conflict. But irreligious societies, such as communism, have created chaos and corruption.

Today both politics and religion need reform. Politicians must become more righteous and spiritual. Religion must become broader and more spiritual to allow freedom of worship and to encompass all the wisdom in the world.

East Dover, Nova Scotia, Canada
June 23, 1999

171

Suppose you go to God, receive a boon, and walk away. When your intention is to get something, then you are in a hurry. A person who knows that he owns God is not in a hurry for anything. Infinite patience arises in him.

When you know you own God, you will not be in a hurry to get something out of God. Your hurry to get something throws you off balance and makes you small. Have infinite patience. When you have infinite patience, you will realize God belongs to you. Either through awareness or through practice you reach the same point.

What does it mean to "own God"? You own God when the Divinity belongs to you. It is not like hurriedly shopping at the supermarket and rushing back home. When you see the whole store is already at home, you are not in a hurry to shop. You are at ease. When you know you are part of the divine plan, you stop demanding. You know that everything is being done for you, that you are taken care of.

To develop patience you need only observe the impatience. Just observe the thoughts and feelings and do not regret them. Usually we do it the other way: we hurry the mind and are slow in our action. Impatience means hurry in the mind; lethargy means slowness in action. Patience in the mind and dynamism in action is the right formula.

Santa Monica, California, United States
August 14, 1996

*T*esting is part of ignorance. You only test that of which you are not sure. If God is testing you, it means God does not know you.

How could you ever think that God is testing you? God does not test you because he knows you completely – your past, present and future. He knows your strengths and weaknesses and He alone gives you strength. He does not test you.

Only you can test yourself. You test yourself only when you do not have confidence. If you are confident, why would you test? If you are testing yourself, you do not know yourself.

Are you testing God? God will never pass your test because He will never show up for it. If He does show up for your test, then He is not God.

European Ashram, Bad Antogast, Germany
January 13, 1999

*T*he Divine has given you all the small pleasures in the world, but has kept bliss to Himself. To get the highest bliss, you have to go to Him and Him alone.

Do not try to be too smart with the Divine and attempt to fool Him. Most of your prayers and rituals are just attempts to trick the Divine. You try to give the least and get the most out of the Divine and He knows this. God is an astute businessman; he will trick you even more. If you go underneath the carpet to find Him, He will go underneath the floor.

Be sincere in your attempts to go to God. Do not try to outsmart the Divine. Once you receive bliss, then everything else is joyful. Without bliss, joy in the world is impermanent.

Montreal Ashram, Quebec, Canada
July 3, 1996

You have always thought of God as a father up in the heavens somewhere. With that concept in mind, you want to demand and take from God. But can you see God as a child? When you see God as a child, you have no demands.

God is the very core of your existence. You are pregnant with God; you must take care of your pregnancy and deliver the child into the world. Most people do not even deliver.

God is your child. God clings to the devotee. He clings to you like a baby until you grow old and die. God keeps crying for nourishment. He needs you to nourish Him in the world. Sadhana, satsang and seva are God's nourishment.

Bangalore Ashram, India
October 16, 1997

*W*hy would you think God is only one? Why cannot God also be many? If God made man in His own image, then what image is He? African, Mongolian, Caucasian, Japanese, Filipino? Why are there so many types of man and so many varieties of things? There is not just one type of tree, not just one type of snake, cloud, mosquito or vegetable. There is not just one type of anything, so why should God be only one?

How could this consciousness that manifested this whole creation and which loves variety, be monotonous? God loves variety, so He must be of infinite variety Himself. God manifests in many names, forms and varieties.

Some schools of thought do not give God the freedom to appear in His many forms. They want Him in one uniform. You change your appearance to suit the occasion, so how can you think there is no variety in the Spirit? Ancient people understood this and that is why they cognized the Divinity as infinite qualities and forms. The Spirit is not dull and boring. The Spirit that is the basis of creation is dynamic and ever-changing. God is not only one, but many.

When you accept the variety of the Divine, you cease to be a fanatic or a fundamentalist.

Dallas, Texas, United States
January 27, 2000

*W*ho wakes up first – you or God? You wake up first, while God is still asleep! When you wake up, you experience pleasure and pain. You become aware of the beauty and the shortcomings of the world. Then, when you seek the ultimate, your cry for help wakes up God, and when God is awakened in you, there is no "two."

The rishis made a mock practice of awakening God every morning. They called it the Suprabhatam service. Many people find this ridiculous because they do not understand the depth of it. But only awakened God can see that God is everywhere asleep. God is asleep in every particle of this universe. God is in you in seed form and when he awakens, neither you nor the world remain.

Curepipe, Mauritius
June 3, 1998

*O*n the day of the full moon at the ancient temple of Kollur an elaborately decorated chariot of the goddess is pulled around the temple. Each one of us is a chariot carrying the power of God within. We are the real chariots of the Divine. Our body is the chariot and our soul is the deity that is pulled around to purify the world.

Bangalore Ashram, India
October 28, 1999

*O*nly that which is temporary, small or perishable needs protection, while that which is permanent, big or vast does not. Protection simply means prolonging the time in a particular state; hence, protection also prevents transformation.

Transformation cannot happen in a state of total protection. At the same time, without protection the desired transformation cannot happen. A seed needs protection to transform into a plant; a plant needs protection to become a tree. But too much protection can aid or hamper transformation, so the protector should have an idea to what extent he should protect.

Both protection and transformation fall within the purview of time and space and these laws have to be honored in order to transcend time. We are both protected and transformed. This is Hari and Hara: Hari, the protector and Hara, the transformer. Protection is limited to time, to perishable things. How long can a doctor heal or protect someone? Forever? No.

Truth does not need any protection. Peace and happiness do not need protection because they are not temporary. Your body needs protection; your soul does not. Your mind needs protection; the Self does not.

Bangalore Ashram, India
August 26, 1999

*T*he Self is not just the mind-body complex. Neither the body nor the mind is the Self. The only purpose for this body to exist is to make you aware of how beautiful you are, and to make you aware that it is possible to live all the values you cherish and create a world of divinity around you. All the yoga asanas you do are for the body. All the meditation you do is for the mind. Whether calm or disturbed, your mind remains mind. Whether sick or well, your body remains body. Self is all-encompassing.

Bangalore Ashram, India
May 16, 1996

*W*hen the body is stimulated, pleasure arises. When your soul is stimulated, love arises. Love has no end, but pleasure ends. Often people think pleasure is love. The distinction between pleasure and love has to be understood; but only the luckiest will understand this.

Just as you eat sugar and stimulate the tongue, music stimulates the ears and sight stimulates the eyes. And what stimulates the soul? Sadhana and satsang are what stimulate the soul.

All we want is stimulation of the soul. Even a faint idea of it keeps life going. Every other stimulus is on the surface. The stimulus of the soul energizes and the stimulus of the body brings fatigue. Every stimulus should lead you to the Self so that when you listen to music, you transcend the music, and when you listen to knowledge it takes you to silence.

European Ashram, Bad Antogast, Germany
January 26, 1999

*S*atyam Param Dhimahi – I uphold in my awareness truth and the Divinity of the transcendental.

The intellect divides the world, and the same intellect can bring it together by soaking itself in Divinity. When the intellect discusses mundane things, it starts dividing existence. When the intellect discusses knowledge, wisdom and truth, then it unites. It brings forth the transcendental. It rediscovers its true nature, which is non-dual.

Whether you complain, compose a poem, or speak knowledge, you are a witness to the flow. When someone complains or justifies, they are simply saying things spontaneously. In the same way, when you speak knowledge of the Self, or spontaneously compose a poem aloud, there is a flow from the intellect.

Anything can flow from the intellect, and you are a witness to the flow, whether it is garbage or wisdom. All that you can do is pray to the Divine, "Let wisdom, divinity and truth flow through this intellect."

Lake Tahoe, California, United States
July 21, 1999

*T*here are five factors that influence the mind: place, time, food, past impressions, and associations and actions.

◆   Every place you are in has a different impact on the mind. Even in your house you can see that you feel differently in different rooms. A place where there has been singing, chanting and meditation has a different influence on the mind than a place where there has been argument or turmoil.

◆   Time is an influence. Different times of the day and year have different influences on the mind.

◆   Different types of food that you eat influence your mind for several days.

◆   Past impressions – karma – have different impacts on the mind. Awareness, alertness, knowledge and meditation help erase past impressions.

◆   Associations and actions, or the people and events with which you are associated, influence your mind. In certain company your mind behaves in one way and with others your mind behaves in a different way.

Though these five factors influence your life and your mind, know that the Self is far more powerful. As you grow in knowledge, you will influence them all.

Milano, Italy
January 6, 2000

*D*esire, action and awareness of the Self are all manifestations of the same energy that is you. Among these three – desire, action and awareness – one dominates at any one time.

When desire dominates, Self-awareness will be at its lowest and stress and sorrow result. That is why philosophers all around the world have advocated renunciation and dropping desires. When action dominates, restlessness and disease are the result. When awareness dominates, happiness dawns. And when your desires and actions are sincerely directed to the welfare of society or to the Divine, then consciousness is automatically elevated, and Self-knowledge is sure to be attained.

Rishikesh, India
March 18, 1999

*T*he Self knows neither sorrow nor death, yet in it flow all relative events.

It is easy to be detached when you are not in love. Being in utter love and yet undisturbed, caring yet not worried, persistent yet not perturbed – all are the obvious signs of the Self shining through.

Bangalore Ashram, India
November 11, 1999

*T*en people were walking on foot from one village to another. On the way, they had to cross a river. Reaching the other shore, they wanted to be sure all had crossed safely. Each one started counting but counted only nine. They became distraught and began to cry for the loss of the tenth.

A wise man came along and asked them, "Oh, my dear friends, why are you crying?"

"We were ten but now we are only nine," they replied.

The wise man saw they were ten, so he asked them to count. Each counted nine but left out himself. Then the wise man made them stand and count off, one by one, and he said to the last person, "You are the tenth!" And they all rejoiced for having regained the tenth.

Similarly the five senses and the four inner faculties – mind, intellect, memory, ego – all lament when they lose sight of the Self. Then the master comes and shows you that you are the tenth! Count, but never stop until you find the tenth. Joy comes with knowledge of the ever-present Self.

Rishikesh, India
March 11, 1998

*A*re you evolving? If you are evolving, you are not in the Self. But you are not out of the Self, because nothing can exist out of the Self.

There are six distortions that do not exist in the Self.

Expansion – Prasarana. Expansion implies there is something into which to expand. That which expands cannot be the basis for expansion.

Contraction – Akunchana. Contraction means something shrinks from something else. Self does not withdraw or shrink from anything, so contraction does not exist in the Self.

Evolution – Vriddhi. Evolution is the process of becoming something that does not already exist. Self is always the same, so it cannot evolve.

Decay – Kshaya. There is no devolution or decay in the Self; it does not get old or stale. That is why when you are close to your Self, you do not feel that you are aging.

Beginning – Anaadi. Self has no beginning. If God has a beginning, then He is not God.

Lack – Abhava. Self has no lack. Whatever lacks something is not complete. Self does not lack anything; it is complete. Lack indicates the existence of something outside itself that does not exist for the Self. So if you feel you have not grown at all, do not worry, you are close to the Self.

When your mind is with the Self, then you do not worry about evolution. If you think about evolving, then you are stuck in the mind. Mind is part of matter, and matter evolves and decays.

That is how the experience of contraction and expansion is all play and display of the mind. Mind expands and contracts. But when it expands, it comes close to the truth, which has no expansion.

European Ashram, Bad Antogast, Germany
January 20, 2000

*H*ow do you become centered? By shifting your awareness from the experience to the one who experiences. All experiences are on the circumference and they are continually changing. The one who experiences is at the center. Again and again come back to the one who experiences.

If you are frustrated, instead of spending your time on the experience of frustration ask, "Who is frustrated?" If you are unhappy ask, "Who is unhappy?" If you think you know something ask, "Who knows it?" If you think you are enlightened ask, "Who is enlightened?" If you think you are ignorant ask, "Who is ignorant?" If you think you are pitiable ask, "Who is poor me?" If you think you are highly devoted ask, "Who is devoted?"

Shed all your faces and face the I. Then you have truly come to me!

Bangalore Ashram, India
September 10, 1997

*L*ife without wisdom is incomplete.
Wisdom that does not give rise to feeling is incomplete.
Feeling that does not translate into action is incomplete.
Action that does not give rise to fulfillment is incomplete.
Fulfillment is returning to the Self.

Bangalore Ashram, India
June 1, 2000

*G*ive me not thirst if you cannot give me water.
Give me not hunger if you cannot give me food.
Give me not joy if I cannot share.
Give me not skills if I cannot put them to good use.
Give me not intelligence if I cannot perceive beyond it.
Give me not knowledge if I cannot digest it.
Give me not love if I cannot serve.
Give me not desires if they do not lead me to you.
Give me not a path if it does not take me home.
Give me not prayers if You will not hear them.

When you pray, to whom do you pray? You pray to yourself. In prayer the mind goes to its source, the Self. God, the master and the Self are the same.

Kauai, Hawaii, United States
April 15, 1999

*A*mong all the planets in the solar system, the earth is privileged to host life in so many forms, and among all the species, humans are the most privileged for they can host the knowledge. Again and again you remember that you are peace, you are love, you are joy and that you are hosting the Creator.

Among all the knowledgeable ones, you are most privileged. Those who do not realize that they are privileged are still hosts, but what they host are negativities. Like birds returning to their nests again and again, come back to your source; only there can you realize that you host the Creator.

Rome, Italy
May 6, 1998

*I*nfinity has diverse qualities and specific qualities assume names – they are called angels.

Angels are simply rays of your big Self. Just as roots and stems come out of a seed as it sprouts, so angels manifest in your life when you are centered. They are there to serve you. Angels are like your extended arms. Just as all the colors are present in white sunlight, all the angels are present in your higher Self. Bliss is their breath; dispassion is their abode.

Shiva is the bestower of dispassion. Shiva is the consciousness that is bliss, innocence and omnipresence. Krishna is the outer manifestation of Shiva and Shiva is the inner silence of Krishna.

Singapore
March 5, 1997

187

*I*t is the intellect that divides and that synthesizes. Some creatures in the world only synthesize and some only divide. Ants only synthesize; they bring things together and build anthills. But monkeys cannot synthesize; they only divide. You give them a garland and they tear it to pieces and throw it all over the place. A monkey can only divide or analyze. A beaver synthesizes, it brings wood together and builds a dam. Birds, such as weaverbirds, also synthesize.

But human beings have both abilities – they analyze and synthesize. You analyze the relative world and synthesize to find the One. The intellect divides to find the truth and truth once found synthesizes everything.

When the intellect becomes quiet, intelligence emerges. Often people think that gathering information makes them intelligent. This is not so. It is samadhi that brings out intelligence. An unintelligent person, in spite of having all information, cannot be creative. An intelligent person, without much information, can be creative.

A sign of intelligence is to see the One in many and find the many in One.

European Ashram, Bad Antogast, Germany
August 27, 1997

*I*f you cannot see the Divine in me, then you need to open your eyes. If you see the Divine in me, then you are a part of me and you cannot be away from me. If you feel a part of me, you can only see the Divine in yourself. If you can see the Divine in yourself, you will see the Divine in everyone.

Kyoto, Japan
November 6, 1996

*M*editation is seeing God in yourself.
Love is seeing God in the person next to you.
Knowledge is seeing God everywhere.
Expression of love is service.
Expression of joy is a smile.
Expression of peace is meditation.
Expressing God is conscious action.

Swargashram (Heavenly Abode), Rishikesh, India
March 13, 1996

*Y*ou only see the fall of water. You do not see how the ocean becomes the cloud. The ocean becoming the cloud is a secret, but the cloud becoming the ocean is obvious.

In the world, only a few can notice your inner growth and height, but your outer expressions are apparent. Never brood that people do not understand you. They can only see your expression.

Look at the water. Even the fall of water is beautiful. If a rock falls it shatters, but when water falls it generates power and beauty. Being somebody is like being a stone; being nobody is like being the water; being everybody is like being water vapor.

Bangalore Ashram, India
September 19, 1996

*E*nlightenment is beyond seasons like the ever green coconut tree.

Sometimes the question arises, "What is the use of all these courses you have taken? Your behavior has not changed!"

The knowledge acquired by a human being cannot be measured or judged by external behavior. Someone may behave as though they have absorbed all the knowledge but internally they have not. The reverse is also true. Someone who seems not to have changed at all may have absorbed a great deal.

Ordinary people just look at the behavior, but the intelligent person looks beyond it and is amazed by the play of consciousness – Brahman.

> Behavior affects relationships.
> Attitude affects behavior.
> Knowledge or ignorance affects attitude.
> Grace brings forth knowledge.

On the inside you are like a tree, in some seasons barren and at other times blossoming. Enlightenment is beyond seasons like the coconut tree that remains green and yields fruit throughout the year.

Bangalore Ashram, India
May 21, 1996

*T*here are three kinds of understanding: intellectual understanding, experiential understanding and existential realization.

Intellectual understanding says "yes" – it agrees. Experiential understanding feels – it is obvious. Existential realization is irrefutable. It becomes your very nature.

If you have only an intellectual understanding, you will think you know everything. Most theologians are in this category. You can know intellectually that you are hollow and empty but sitting and feeling you are hollow and empty is totally different. All that you hear will simply remain a jumble of words if there is no experiential understanding, which is more on the feeling level. When you have an experience, you want to understand more about it and so you become a seeker. Existential realization contains within it both experiential and intellectual understanding yet it is beyond both of these. How do you achieve existential realization? There is no way to achieve it. When the fruit becomes ripe, it falls.

Montreal Ashram, Quebec, Canada
October 14, 1998

*Y*ou have many faces; only you do not face them. From time to time in different phases of your life, different faces appear. When you confront your faces then conflicts, confusion and chaos arise in you. But as you come close to your being, all the faces melt and leave you as the space that you are.

At the gross level, you identify yourself as someone. At a subtle level, you identify yourself as energy or as an incarnation of an angel, saint or prophet. But when you go beyond even this identity, you are whole, holy, Brahman – Purna Brahman Narayana.

Bangalore Ashram, India
December 18, 1997

*S*hiva is called Chandrasekhara, which means "that mind which is in Shiva – transcendence – and is always above the peak."

Buddha is not on the peak; rather the peak is beneath Buddha. One who goes to the mountain comes down, but the mountain seeks the one who is stationed in inner space.

Hong Kong
October 31, 1996

*C*onsciousness moving on the surface of the body is stimulus, which causes pleasure. When consciousness shrinks or contracts, then pain and suffering arise. When consciousness moves through the body in limited channels, pleasure is experienced.

Repeated enjoyment of stimuli causes inertia and dullness. Often cooks do not enjoy their own food. The same piece of music heard over and over again loses its charm. People in the sex industry do not enjoy sex.

If stimuli are observed, then consciousness expands and becomes peace. With awareness the stimuli lose their significance; whether they exist or not makes no difference. When the sun is shining, it makes no difference if the candle is lit or not. To realize that all pleasures are just stimuli and that you are more than the stimuli brings freedom.

Pain is nothing but consciousness wanting to expand and to become free. Freedom is liberation from the craving of stimuli. Pain is not a permanent state. Like the insomniac who has forgotten how to sleep, most of us have forgotten how to be at peace and in bliss. Just as the natural tendency of water is to flow downward, and the natural tendency of air is not to be under pressure, the natural tendency of consciousness is to expand and be at peace.

Hamburg, Germany
August 26, 1998

*R*a in Sanskrit means that which is radiant and "ma" means myself.

That which shines forth within me is Rama. That which is radiant in every particle of my being is Rama.

Rama was born to Dasharatha and Kaushalya. Dasharatha means "the ten-charioted one" in Sanskrit. It signifies the five sense organs and the five organs of action. Kaushalya is Sanskrit for "skilled." The skillful driver of the ten chariots can give birth to Rama. When the five sense organs and the five organs of action are used skillfully, radiance is born within.

Rama was born in Ayodhya, which in Sanskrit means "the place where no war can happen." When there is no conflict in our mind, then radiance can dawn.

Lakshmana, the brother of Rama, was born of Sumitra – the good friend. When the five sense organs and five organs of action are cooperating within you, awareness is born and you become radiant. Often we try to look within for radiance. Just realize that you are radiant.

Bangalore, India
April 13, 2000

Often people say, "Be the same outside as you are inside." But I ask you, how is this possible?

Inside you are a vast ocean, an infinite sky. Outside you are finite – just a small limited form, a normal stupid person with limitations and faults.

All that you are inside – the love, the beauty, the compassion, the Divinity – does not show up fully outside. What shows outside is only the crust of behaviors.

Ask yourself, am I really my behavioral patterns? Am I really this limited body-mind complex? No. You are not the same inside as outside. Do not mistake the outer crust for what you are inside. And do not show your infinite lordship outside, for Divinity is not easily understood. Let there be some mystery.

Rishikesh, India
March 19, 1998

*W*hen knowledge is lodged in you as wisdom, it will never leave you. Wisdom lodges itself in your heart.

Make the Divine your sweet Beloved. This is the first thing to do and the last thing to do.

Keep your heart in a safe place; it is too delicate. Events, small things make strong impressions on it. You cannot find a better place than the Divine to keep your heart safe and your mind sane. When you keep your heart in the Divine, moving time and passing events will not be able to touch it; they will not create a scar.

A precious stone needs a gold or silver setting around it to hold it and to keep it safe as you wear it; so wisdom and knowledge are the setting around the heart that will hold it in the Divine.

Fort Lauderdale, Florida, United States
February 12, 1997

*B*lessings come to you in many forms.

Make your home God's home and there will be light, love and abundance.

Make your body God's abode and there will be peace and bliss.

Feel your mind is a toy of God and you will watch and enjoy all its games.

See this world as play and as a display of God Himself and you will repose in the non-dual Self.

If you are generous, blessing comes to you as abundance.

If you are hard-working, blessing comes to you as happiness.

If you are lazy, blessing comes to you as hard work.

If you are pleasure-loving, blessing comes to you as dispassion.

If you are dispassionate, blessing comes to you as knowledge of the Self.

European Ashram, Bad Antogast, Germany
May 13, 1999

*T*ime and space are infinite. Grains of sand are countless. Atoms in the universe are innumerable as are the stars and the galaxies.

There is neither a beginning nor an end because everything is spherical. A sphere has no beginning and no end, no goal or direction.

Truth has no direction, no goal. Truth itself is the goal, and truth is infinite.

Feeling and experiencing infinity within this finite body, living timelessness within the time span of life, uncovering bliss within misery – this is what you are here for.

When wisdom dawns, it gives rise to celebration. But in celebration you may lose your focus, your awareness. The ancient rishis knew this, so to maintain awareness amidst the gaiety of celebration, they brought sacredness and puja to every event.

Rishikesh, India
October 30, 1997

Some questions can only be answered in silence. Silence is the goal of all answers. If an answer does not silence the mind, it is no answer.

Thoughts are not the goal in themselves. Their goal is silence. When you ask the question "who am I?" you get no answer, there is only silence. That is the real answer. Your soul is solidified silence and this solidified silence is wisdom, knowledge.

The easy way to silence thoughts is to arouse feelings, for only through feelings will peace, joy and love dawn. They are all your very nature.

To the question "who am I?" the only relevant answer is silence. You need to discard all answers in words, including "I am nothing" or "I am the cosmic self" or "I am the Self." Just remain with the question "who am I?" All other answers are just thoughts and thoughts can never be complete.

Only silence is complete.

Rishikesh, India
March 16, 2000

Sri Sri Ravi Shankar

*S*ri Sri is a renowned saint from an ancient lineage of masters of Southern India. In 1982, Sri Sri began to teach the Sudarshan Kriya, a powerful breathing technique that eliminates stress and brings one completely into the present moment. Today this is part of the popular Art of Living Course taught around the world. People have found powerful, long-lasting relief from the stresses and strains of their lives and have gained an unshakable sense of balance and joy.

Sri Sri Ravi Shankar is the founder of the Art of Living Foundation, a United Nations Non-Governmental Organization, and is the founder or inspiration behind numerous other charitable activities for service and the promotion of human values. As Sri Sri has said, "Service is the expression of joy and love. Ask yourself, 'How can I be useful to those around me and to the whole world?' Then your heart starts to blossom and a completely new level begins…"

Each year Sri Sri travels around the world, invited to speak at large and small institutions reminding us that the great spiritual traditions have common goals and values, and that we are here to enjoy, to grow and to contribute. Sri Sri is certainly the epitome of these human qualities, these human values.

The **Art of Living Foundation** is an international nonprofit educational and humanitarian organization that offers workshops for self-development and spiritual growth that allow busy people to take advantage of Sri Sri's multidimensional teachings. The Art of Living Foundation is a Non-Governmental Organization (NGO) with the United Nations and sponsors service projects worldwide, including programs for people living with HIV, cancer, and depression, rehabilitative training for prisoners and vocational training for rural people in Asia.

The **Art of Living Course** is the ideal introduction to Sri Sri's wisdom. This 16-18 hour program over 6 days has uplifted the lives of many people worldwide. Breath contains the secret of life. Breath is linked to the vital life energy in us, or prana. Low prana translates into depression, lethargy, dullness and poor enthusiasm. When the mind and body are charged with prana, we feel alert, energetic and joyful. Specific breathing techniques revitalize and invigorate our physical and emotional well-being. You learn several powerful breathing practices, including Sudarshan Kriya, a unique process that fully oxygenates the cells, recharging them with new energy and life. Negative emotions stored as toxins in the body are naturally flushed out. Tension, anger, anxiety, depression and lethargy are released and forgotten. The mind is left calm and centered, with a clearer vision of the world, our relationships and ourselves. The workshop also includes processes and deep insights into the nature of life and how to live happily and artfully. To take this workshop contact the Art of Living Center nearest you, see the directory on page 206 or visit www.artofliving.org.

Advanced Courses are for those who have completed the Art of Living Course. These retreats spent in silence provide a profound opportunity to explore the depths of your own inner silence through deep meditation, seva and special processes. Each evening ends with a celebration of singing, dancing and wisdom. You leave feeling renewed and elevated, with a dynamism for greater success in all your activities. Some Advanced Courses are offered in Sri Sri's presence – meeting the master personally is a profound experience.

Sahaj Samadhi Meditation. Not one of us lacks spiritual depth. The peace and happiness we seek in the world are already contained within us, covered only by clouds of stress and strain. These clouds are lifted with Sahaj Samadhi Meditation, a gift from Sri Sri. Sahaj Samadhi Meditation provides a rest much deeper than sleep. Like awakening renewed on a sunny morning, your outlook on life becomes more positive. Stress drops off, the chattering mind becomes serene and creative, aging slows and you rediscover the unshakable contentment of your inner Self. Sahaj Samadhi Meditation is easy to learn and practice. With simple guidance, anyone can meditate. Personal instruction is offered at Art of Living Centers worldwide.

ART Excel – All 'Round Training for Excellence – is a course for children and teens, providing practical techniques that enable young people to handle negative emotions such as fear, anger and frustration in positive ways. Taught on the ART Excel Course are vital non-academic skills such as the art of making friends, the secret of popularity, and the value of service to others – all in a supportive, yet challenging and fun atmosphere. Our toughest critics – the kids themselves – give this program rave reviews.

Prison SMART (Stress Management and Rehabilitative Training) **Foundation, Inc.** is an innovative program licensed to teach a variation of the Art of Living Course in correctional facilities and juvenile detention centers in the United States.

You can learn more about these programs at:
www.artofliving.org

Books, videotapes, and audiotapes of Sri Sri are available by mail. Titles include: God Loves Fun, The Path of Love, Compassion and Trust, The Purpose of Life, The Ultimate Relationship, Om Shanti Shanti Shanti and the Yoga Sutras of Patanjali.

For a catalog of products and to order, contact:

Art of Living Books and Tapes
(800) 574-3001 U.S.A. or (641) 472-9892
Facsimile: (641) 472-0671
E-mail: aolmailorder@lisco.com

The Art of Living Foundation's sister organization, the **International Association for Human Values (IAHV)** provides humanitarian service projects. **5H** – Health, Homes, Hygiene, Human Values, and Harmony in Diversity – is the primary service arm of IAHV. 5H provides tools and resources to address not only basic human needs but also to foster individual empowerment and harmony in communities. The unique approach for 5H begins with its innovative Youth Training Program (YTP) which trains young people to become 5H community service leaders with a special emphasis on human values and sensitivity to cultural diversity and traditions. IAHV's **Homes for Changes** program – an element of 5H – is building homes, wells, and septic systems for poor families in India. For more information visit www.5h.org and www.iahv.org.

Care for Children provides children with food, clothing and education. It is also building new schools in areas where they are needed and rebuilding schools in Gujarat, India after the 2001 earthquake. It began as the **Dollar-a-Day** program supporting a rural school in Bangalore, India, the only school of its kind in the area and grew to house and serve boys and girls from 50 surrounding villages. The approach used for this first school is expanding to other areas of India. All services are administered at no charge to each child. To learn more about this program, go to www.careforchildren.org or look under "Service" at www.artofliving.org.

AFRICA
Hema & Rajaraman
Art of Living
P.O. Box 1213
Peba Close Plot 5612
Gaborone, Botswana
Tel. 26-735-2175
aolbot@global.co.za

CANADA
Art of Living Foundation
P.O. Box 170
13 Infinity Rd.
Saint-Mathieu-du-Parc
Quebec G0X 1N0
Canada
Tel. 819-532-3328
artofliving.northamerica@
sympatico.ca

GERMANY
Akadamie Bad Antogast
Bad Antogast 1
77728 Oppenau
Germany
Tel. 49-7804-910-923
artofliving.germany@
t-online.de

INDIA
Vyakti Vikas Kendra, India
No. 19, 39th A Cross,
11th Main
4th T Block, Jayanagar
Bangalore 560041, India
Tel. 91-80-6645106
vvm@vsnl.com

UNITED STATES
Art of Living Foundation
P.O. Box 50003
Santa Barbara, CA 93150
Tel. 805-564-1002
U.S. toll free: 877-399-1008
www.artofliving.org